Your

God-

Given

Potential

Also by Winifred Wilkinson Hausmann

Focus on Living
Miracle Power for Today
How to Live Life Victoriously
Dealing With Stress Through Spiritual Methods
A Guide to Love-Powered Living

Unfolding Your God-Given Potential

the Twelve Spiritual Powers

Winifred Wilkinson Hausmann

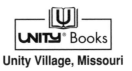

UNITY® Books

Unity Village, Missouri

Revised Paperback Edition 1999

Copyright © 1978, 1999 by Unity School of Christianity. All rights re-
served. No part of this book may be used or reproduced in any manner
whatsoever without written permission except in the case of brief quotations embodied in critical articles and reviews or in the newsletters and
lesson plans of licensed Unity teachers and ministers. For information, ad-
dress Unity Books, Publishers, Unity School of Christianity, 1901 NW
Blue Parkway, Unity Village, MO 64065-0001.

To receive a catalog of all Unity publications (books, cassettes, compact
discs, and magazines) or to place an order, call our Customer Service Department: (816) 969-2069 or 1-800-669-0282.

Cover Design by Gretchen West
Cover Photograph by Neal and Molly Jansen/SuperStock

Library of Congress Cataloging-in-Publication Data
Hausmann, Winifred Wilkinson.
    Your God-given potential : unfolding the twelve spiritual powers /
Winifred Wilkinson Hausmann. — Rev. pbk. ed.
        p.   cm.
    ISBN 0-87159-213-4
    1. Christian life—Unity School of Christianity authors.
I. Title.
BV4501.2.H3675   1998
248.4'8997—dc21   98-41336
Canada BN 13252 9033 RT   CIP

Unity Books feels a sacred trust to be a healing presence in the world. By
printing with biodegradable soybean ink on recycled paper, we believe we
are doing our part to be wise stewards of our Earth's resources.

Publisher's Note:

Throughout this book there are numerous quotations from the writings of Charles Fillmore, Unity's co-founder. For the convenience of readers, the sources of these are provided in the following abbreviated forms.

TM	*The Twelve Powers*
RW	*The Revealing Word*
MG	*Mysteries of Genesis*
TT	*Talks on Truth*
MBD	*Metaphysical Bible Dictionary*
ASP	*Atom-Smashing Power of Mind*
MJ	*Mysteries of John*

Bible quotations are taken from the Revised Standard Version unless otherwise noted. Quoted word definitions are taken from *Webster's New World Dictionary.*

Table

of Contents

Foreword
to the
1999 Edition

I have spent over twenty years in research and in-depth teaching of Charles Fillmore's concept of the twelve powers—nine years teaching it at Unity Ministerial School and fourteen in the Continuing Education Program of USRS. I have not found a better book for the novice than Winifred Wilkinson Hausmann's *Your God-Given Potential.* It is easy to follow and yet manages to carry great depth.

On a personal note, I have known Winifred and her late husband George for many years. In fact, when my husband Frank and I left our ministry in Pittsburgh, Pennsylvania, to begin our work at Unity Village, Missouri, Winifred became our interim minister. So it is a great pleasure for me to write this foreword and welcome back into print this important book.

The title of Winifred Hausmann's book *Your God-Given Potential* captures our attention and makes us desirous of knowing what that potential is and how we can tap into its power. Here is a very practical text that offers specific guidelines for

1

building a personal program of spiritual development for anyone wanting to achieve such a goal.

In this mind-stretching book, Winifred shows you how—with inner guidance—you can change your thinking, expand your consciousness, and remake your personal world. Focusing on twelve divinely given powers within us, she offers an in-depth understanding of each of the powers, which are the source of our God-given potential, and how they unfold in consciousness.

Each chapter concludes with seven powerful steps that enable us to accept each concept presented, make it a part of our understanding, and reach spiritual attunement with the power. Statements at the end of each chapter are excellent tools for consciousness conditioning through daily affirmation and times of meditation.

The message of the book, though simply stated, is profound and deeply challenging. It is designed to bring new revelations to the beginner and add deeper insights for study by the long-time Truth student. My personal credo, "You have the power and the power is within you," is fully revealed in this extraordinary book.

Martha V. Giudici

April 1998

An ordained Unity minister since 1967, Martha V. Giudici coministered, with her husband Frank, the Unity Village Chapel for many years. She also taught in the ministerial education and the continuing education programs of both Unity Ministerial School and Unity School for Religious Studies. Her postgraduate study of the twelve powers, a teaching guide to Charles Fillmore's *Christian Healing,* is still in print with the Association of Unity Churches.

Introduction

Since we humans began paying attention to other creatures, we have been intrigued by their innate abilities. We admire the strength of the elephant, the cunning of the lion, the camel's ability to travel on the hot desert, and the migratory abilities of birds.

It is good to admire the God-given abilities in all forms of life. But shouldn't we be giving more time and attention to our own God-given potentiality? What other creature can adapt to any environment—in the tropics, in frigid areas, under the sea, or even on the moon?

Think of it: Without the specific abilities of other forms of life, with little or none of the instinct that we admire in animals, we can, through the use of our mind power alone, duplicate any of the animals' feats and do it in any environment.

It is probably true that primitive people had to migrate with the seasons and the food supply. But it was not long before they brought mind power into play to bring food to them, to adapt

3

by using fire and clothes to keep warm, and to make other necessary adjustments.

The prediction in Genesis was that we would have dominion over all things, and we are beginning to fulfill that prediction. We have saved some endangered species from extinction, and we have caused others to become extinct. We have both used and misused our environment. We have learned to cross- and interbreed all kinds of animals, plants, flowers, and trees to produce a desired result. And, in our physical universe, this is just the beginning!

No other creature on our planet—no matter how great—can do what human beings can do; and we can do it only because of our developed faculties of imagination, understanding, will, and zeal. Untold accomplishments of the future are also contained in the divine potential of our God-given faculties.

We have reached the moon. There is a vast universe out there beyond the moon. But the greatest adventure awaits us within our own being, as we begin to recognize that the dominion God promised us in the beginning is not simply the dominion over our environment or over the lower forms of life, but the dominion we are to exercise over our own attributes. This dominion is to be exercised not only on the mental plane, but also in the area of spiritual development. No matter how completely we subdue our physical world, we will forever be restless until we become the "light of the world" (Mt. 5:14) that Jesus sought to call forth in every one of us.

This book is designed to enable the reader to recognize the twelve spiritual powers with which God has endowed us all—

to recognize them and to develop them under that spiritual pattern, the Christ of our nature, which is the greatest gift of all.

—George R. Hausmann
1978

From Primordial Cell to Christ-Oriented Human

Arecent medical survey showed that the most frequent health complaint is the common, everyday headache. The headache is so common in our modern society that it is often the butt of comedians' jokes. It provides an acceptable excuse for everything, from missing a day of work to leaving a party early. In some circles the person who never has a headache (or a medical bill) is considered peculiar.

Why is this? Why is the headache so common a physical difficulty, and why is the fact of its existence so widely accepted? Why do so many people suffer from this complaint? With an understanding of our *twelve powers* and their locations in the body, we can easily see the answer to these questions. When we come to understand these powers and their relationship to our physical well-being, we have a significant key to the healing of problems of mind and manifestation.

Consider the head area: Four of our twelve attributes work from centers in the cranial area. These are the four powers that are exclusive with human beings, the products of the increasing complexity which has characterized our evolutionary process. Animals and other lower forms of life express such qualities as strength, instinctive intelligence, elimination, and order. But even the most highly developed animal cannot boast imagination or faith. Only we human beings, with our God-given ability to think and choose, have acquired the powers of *faith, imagination, understanding,* and *will.* Only we can decide to misuse these gifts of God and suffer the results in the form of a physical reaction in the part of the body where the faculties are located: the head. Only humans can have headaches.

When we learn to recognize the cause and bring about a change in our thinking-feeling nature, we can correct the difficulty. A study of our twelve attributes not only enables us to develop them mentally, physically, and spiritually, it also gives us keys to healing the mind, body, and affairs. To gain a greater insight into our powers and the centers they inhabit, let us take a look at the evolutionary process as it unfolded the physical expressions of these twelve soul qualities.

Our planet Earth started as a whirling, seething mass of gases. Gradually, through various processes of condensation, volcanic eruptions, slow seepage, chemicalization, and other orderly changes, the earth was prepared for the first appearance of life. As the planet cooled, coagulated, and produced a friendly atmosphere, according to modern scientific belief, an infinitesimal form appeared. This tiny primordial cell had the attribute of *life* and, presumably, a life center, which enabled it to reproduce and perpetuate its line in the way that was right and proper for it. Cell division, its method of reproduction, was different from that of humans, but the life idea was there. There had to be an expression of life, however simple, to keep the cell alive in the first place and to continue the process of evolution.

Two other powers must also have come into being with that first tiny organism. While we could not say the first cell had wisdom, it certainly had its own brand of *intelligence,* a built-in, instinctive knowing that directed its life activity and taught it how to survive and perpetuate its species.

Love, "the power that joins and binds in divine harmony the universe and everything in it" (*RW,* pp. 124-125), was also present and active in that first tiny cell. At some point the love power began to work as what is sometimes referred to now as "altruistic selfishness." As the cell multiplied itself on earth, survival became a precarious business. The answer was for the cells to combine, expressing a sort of unselfish selfishness. This strengthened the individual components and gave them a greater ability to cope with life in their world, and so they brought forth the forms that were the next step up in the evolutionary process.

The three early powers, *life; intelligence;* and *love,* or attraction—continued to be a part of all life forms and to guide and motivate the production of increasingly complex organisms and the survival of those most adaptable to the evolutionary process.

Strength became a more and more prominent quality as the organisms grew, and with the advent of the vertebrates, it even acquired a center, or location, in the spinal column. Strength was tremendously important during the many long years in which survival of the fittest was the norm. Life forms that were weak simply could not continue to exist. The prevailing mode of survival of the fittest resulted in the strengthening of some lines and the elimination of others.

Because of this method of perpetuating the species most able to cope with the environmental and physical stresses, another of our qualities came into prominence. Throughout the history of developing life forms on this planet, there was an activity of elimination, or *renunciation*. Always the less strong, the less competent, gave way to the greater, stronger fish, bird, or animal. Nature's process of getting rid of the feeble or deficient animals was, in effect, a contribution to the survival of life itself. Without the important activity of elimination, our planet would long since have become so overcrowded that *all* would have perished.

Because the whole universe is under God's law and operates according to universal principles, a necessary quality in the developing life forms was *order.* This enabled the fish, bird, or animal to adapt to its environment, learn to live with members of its species, and relate to other groups as well. The earliest form of life that crawled out of the sea and gradually adapted to living on land had to employ some sort of order. And, in a very real sense, the whole evolutionary process is an activity of divine order, an unfolding of more and more complex organisms through many generations of selective survival. Without the faculty of order, there would be no survival.

These six qualities that played such an important part in the history of the evolution of living organisms (*life, intelligence, love, strength, elimination,* and *order*) are still important today. They are important to us because they are the powers that operate in the subconscious area of our being, from body centers. These powers, which are focalized below the neck area, are highly individualized and developed. They are the qualities that guided the unfolding strain from the first tiny primordial cell to the most intelligent, competent animal-survivor of the evolutionary process.

An understanding of these powers and their locations in the body will contribute to our healing abilities. All these powers, developed under the guidance of Spirit, will take us into new realms never dreamed of in our present stage of evolving the "new creation" individual of the future. The awakening of strength, for instance, through its ganglionic center in the small of the back, automatically strengthens the whole person. As stability of purpose flows into the mind, the idea of physical endurance brings its reaction into all the muscles of the body, and on the level that is exclusive with human beings, spiritual strength reinforces the whole direction of life itself.

In the neck are the centers for two attributes that operate somewhere between the conscious and subconscious levels, unless consciously directed. The home of power at the root of the tongue, closely associated with the larynx (and the vocal cords), may be directed either by subconscious reaction or by conscious, creative command.

Consider the higher animal forms that have a power center. All of their activity is from the level of instinctive behavior. A dog barks, a lion roars, or a donkey brays; it does not stop to think about it. The sound simply comes out in response to a particular stimulus—hunger, fright, or some other basic goal.

Only humans have developed the power center as a means for communicating what we think. (And sometimes we react automatically to an outer stimulus, speaking before we think.) But the quality is there. Undoubtedly, at some point we began to develop our power center because of a need to communicate, one of the products of the developing power of thought. Perhaps at first we indicated our wants with grunts, but as the power of conscious thought developed, we began to use our vocal cords to express pleasure or pain and, finally, our new-found ability to think and reason. It is well for all of us to remember that in using this God-given attribute, we must be conscious of what we are saying. If we are not, our subconscious may take over and respond before we know what we are doing. How many healing needs in human relationships are the result of words that never should have been said!

The other borderline power (between conscious and subconscious) is *zeal,* working from its throne in the back of the neck. Charles Fillmore describes zeal as "the urge behind all things" (*TM,* p. 130) and "the affirmative impulse of existence" (*TM,* p. 132). Something—some force, some impelling activity—is in and through all things and behind all growth and development. In human beings this is partly a subconscious urge and partly a conscious enthusiasm. Lower forms of life have to respond to the impulse that controls their destiny; only humans can think about it. Only we may choose the direction zeal will take us, even though sometimes our enthusiasm becomes so insistent that we follow without thinking. Zeal is energy. Zeal carries its own power to accomplish. But zeal must be consciously directed, if it is to serve well.

Somewhere in the evolutionary process, in a way that no scientist has ever been able to explain, a new life form came forth. To a certain degree, human beings had physical characteristics similar to some of the animals; but we were not animals. We had a quality that had hitherto been missing on the earth—the power of conscious, reflective thought. This new human form of life not only continued to use the powers previously exercised by the animals, but also developed exclusive attributes.

Animals "know" many things in their store of instinctive intelligence, but they do not know that they know. They cannot even choose their environment; they adapt or they die.

The human mind has subconscious powers with centers in the body—the borderline qualities working from areas in the neck and also the very special attributes of faith, imagination, will, and understanding—our own exclusive servants, reigning from their thrones in the cranium. Not only that, but we have something even more important—the spiritual pattern for the development of our innate potentiality. From the very top of the head, shedding its light in and through all the power centers as it is invited to do, the *Christ center* provides guidance, direction, and reinforcement for the development of all our powers and abilities.

It is a part of divine planning that the Christ center, while it pours out its spiritual activity in and through all twelve gan-glionic locations, is actually closest to the four conscious pow-ers that are located in the head, the product of the increasing complexity of the organism.

Perhaps the earliest conscious quality that we developed was the power of the *imagination,* the ability to picture in our mind. Animals can be taught to imitate and to do various tricks, but only *we* can invent, and we invent by using our imaging fac-ulty. Archaeologists searching for remnants of early man may have difficulty in sorting out some of the evidence, but if they find tools, they know that human beings were there. Animals may use the parts of their bodies to dig, tear, eat, and kill. But only humans, because of their inner vision, can invent a tool.

Imagination functions as a third eye, actually interpreting and reporting what is seen. Suppose we see a stick. Our thought orientation, backed up by our power of imagination, may in-terpret it as firewood. A carpenter may mentally make a small figure from it. The conservationist may use it as a reminder of the depleted supplies of natural resources. Somewhere along the line, prehistoric people looked at a stick and saw it as a tool, something that would enable them to dig or break open or push or pull. The development of the imaging power, with its center between the eyes, marked a great step forward in the evolution of the thinking, feeling human being.

With the advent of these mental powers centered in the head, the survival of the fittest took on a new meaning in evolution. It no longer referred to brawn, but to brains. Developing men-tal attributes not only enabled us to adapt in our environment, but also to change our environment and to outwit or mentally dominate the lower forms of life.

Early humans, with their receding foreheads, showed little development of the twin faculties of understanding and will, both in the front-brain area. But gradually, as they used reflective thought to figure things out, they filled out this area of the head, creating a center for understanding. As they started to make decisions and take command of their lives and affairs, they developed a throne for will. This actually changed their physical appearance more than any other single development since humans began to walk upright.

Animals acted on instinct. Developing humans began to act on faith. They developed habits, based on the faith that certain things were true. We continue to develop habits of thinking and acting, all according to our faith.

These four most complex attributes, a part of our consciousness, must be used always under the guidance and direction of the Christ, shedding light from the center nearby in the crown of the cranium.

Allowed to work purely from human direction, the determined will causes one form of the common complaint, the headache. Attempting to force intellectual understanding can also bring pain to the front forehead. Misdirected faith is another offender; and imagined ills, hurts, and troubles not only express themselves as pain in the affected area, but also as problems of sight.

With the advent of human life came the four conscious powers and the ability to become the Christ-oriented individual of the future—an individual with power completely developed according to the image and likeness of God, which was implanted in the beginning.

We have the ability to command our faculties. We can think about ourselves and our world. We can consciously relate to our environment or change it. In our highest development, we also have the key to the next step in our evolutionary process: we have the Christ within, pouring all radiance in and through our whole being from the Christ throne at the crown of the head.

Under Christ direction, we can be healed. More than that—we can become "fourth dimensional," the "new creation," the Christ-oriented individuals of the future.

Discover a New World Within

Jesus Christ, our Elder Brother and Way-Shower, spoke positive, powerful words about the potential within him— and the God-given potentiality within every person.

On several occasions Jesus indicated a potentiality above and beyond even the wonderful powers he was expressing. He declared in John 16:15, "All that the Father has is mine," and he spoke authoritatively of "greater works" that would be done by others who followed in his way.

Our work here and now is to awaken to the divine powers with which God has endowed us, to encourage and develop them under God's direction and to get about the business of becoming what Jesus demonstrated in his life and told us we could become. Look at it this way:

You have within you a supply of latent energy that is limited only by your ability to believe, conceive, and develop it. Spirit, soul, and body, you are endowed with capabilities that are only now beginning to be discovered and called forth by humankind. This is the potential that was given to you, His beloved child, by God, in the beginning, "before the world was made."

Jesus called it forth. He expressed perfectly his spiritual attributes in mind and body, and so can you. One of Jesus' last instructions to us, his followers, was, "Follow me" (Jn. 21:19).

Within each person there is a new world awaiting discovery, a world in which there are capabilities of unlimited strength, perfect knowing, radiant life, and other latent abilities beyond our greatest present capacity to conceive. Even our quality of imagination must be developed to enable us to glimpse the potentiality with which God has endowed us.

This is the world of the "new creation" person projected by the apostle Paul and the "fourth dimension man" foreseen by Unity co-founder Charles Fillmore. Our work, as seekers of a new age, is to bring this new person into manifestation. We do it by developing and expressing, in greater and greater degrees, our God-given potential.

More than sixty years ago, Charles Fillmore gave the world his blueprint for the person of this new era. He introduced the concept with the admonition that the "spiritual quickening of man [male and female] on the human plane and his transformation into the divine" would be brought about "not by a miracle or the fiat of God, but by the gradual refinement of the man of flesh into the man of Spirit" (*TM*, p. 4).

Fillmore's plan for the regeneration of humankind was based on the individual development of innate powers and abilities expressing themselves through ganglionic centers in the human body. These centers are to be activated as the qualities are developed in mind, all under the supervision of the Christ or God Self of each person.

The centers are symbolized by the twelve disciples of Jesus, and those who seek to develop the powers or faculties are reminded that all must be evolved under the guidance and direction of the Christ. The disciples were developed by Jesus from ordinary working men into dedicated apostles and were entrusted with the mission of spreading the Jesus Christ teaching on earth.

Twelve is the mystical number of perfection. The twelve tribes of Israel were the progeny of the twelve sons of Jacob. They represent twelve faculties of humanity in an earlier, more primitive state. In the disciples of Jesus, we find the twelve again, this time more highly developed and more clearly defined.

If we would develop these twelve qualities in ourselves, we must study the faculties, relate to their physical centers in our body in an enlightened way, and let them grow through prayer and attention. However, we must remember always to keep them under the direction of the Christ, our own spiritual nature.

Under no circumstances should we develop the powers simply for our personal gain or to exercise personal power over other people. In the study of the twelve powers, we are entering into the next step of our evolutionary process on earth, and if we do not handle our evolving potential in the right way, we may be destroyed by it.

Fillmore warns: "The electronic energy in man is a form of

fire, which is represented by Gehenna. This electronic fire must be used unselfishly. If used to further the selfishness of man, it becomes destructive, through the crosscurrents that it sets up in the nervous system" (*TM,* p. 6).

Used positively, this power can be a force for good beyond anything we have experienced. Our work as individuals is to activate something that is above and beyond our human powers. When we, through the Christ, awaken the endowment God gave us in the beginning, we are literally calling forth the positive, powerful current of the God-idea within us that is unlimited.

This book is not designed to replace Charles Fillmore's explanation of the twelve powers, which is as timely today as it was when *The Twelve Powers of Man* was first published in 1930. It is, rather, designed to present a practical, step-by-step guide to developing our God-given potential, for those who are inspired to be forerunners in the evolution of the individual of the new millennium.

The centers in the body are to be activated for the purpose of gaining a greater experience of each power, but it must be remembered that the powers are developed only secondarily in the body. The primary consideration is to expand the conscious awareness of each quality in the soul nature and to do it all under Christ dominion. Each individual starts where he or she is in soul unfoldment and grows in ability to use and express the powers as concentrated attention is given to the program of development.

Our work is to transmute the natural powers (starting where

we are in consciousness and spiritual growth) into the spiritual powers we are designed to express for the fulfillment of our Christ potential. Each faculty is discovered first as an intellectual concept. This concept is explored and nurtured through prayer as it gradually grows into the spiritual idea from which it came. Finally we have no sense of separateness, but rather a realization of our oneness with the God-power itself, expressing itself through us entirely under the guidance and direction of the Christ. Then, and only then, we are ready for the next giant step in the evolutionary process of humankind.

Remember, each power functions in three ways—first, the perfect idea in Divine Mind; second, the growing concept in our consciousness; third, the expression through the physical center and (indirectly) through our entire body. The long-range goal is to attain a complete and perfect expression of all twelve powers through all phases of our being. This would be the fulfilling realization of oneness with our Creator. We believe that Jesus reached and demonstrated this oneness.

Although we do not develop the faculties simply for the realization of physical power, we find that as a bonus we will begin to experience greater physical power as we grow in consciousness. Our aim is not simply to build greater mind power, but with that power we will gain a new and greater sense of spiritual knowing and illumination in all our mental activities. Our highest aim, that of learning to express our spiritual nature, will pay the greatest dividends in soul satisfaction and discovery of the meaning of life here on earth.

Paul explained the unfoldment of our God-given potential

in this way: "It is sown a physical body, it is raised a spiritual body. If there is a physical body, there is also a spiritual body. Thus it is written, 'The first man Adam became a living being'; the last Adam became a life-giving spirit. But it is not the spiritual which is first but the physical, and then the spiritual. The first man was from the earth, a man of dust; the second man is from heaven. . . . Just as we have borne the image of the man of dust, we shall also bear the image of the man of heaven" (1 Cor. 15:44-47, 49).

The aggregation of cells that is to serve as the director of development for all the powers is the I Am or Christ center at the top or crown of the head. From this vantage point at the apex of the body, the Christ sends its rays of light to the focal points of the twelve faculties, guiding their development and growth in consciousness.

Based on the system developed by Charles Fillmore, the ganglionic centers in the body, the powers they control, and the disciples who represent them are:

The Twelve Centers

The *faith* center is in the *middle of the head, in the area of the pineal gland.* To locate the center, draw an imaginary line between the ears and cross it with imaginary lines from the eyes, intersecting in the middle. The point in the middle, where the imaginary lines converge, is the headquarters of your faith faculty. Faith is represented by the disciple *Simon Peter.*

Strength, closely allied with the activity of the *adrenal glands,* is located in the *small of the back. Andrew* is the disciple for strength.

Wisdom makes its abode at the *pit of the stomach* and is closely allied to the function of the *pancreas.* Its disciple is *James, the son of Zebedee.*

Love works from its center at the *back of the heart. John, the son of Zebedee,* who has been described as the disciple whom Jesus loved, represents this quality. Since James and John are brothers, the centers of love and wisdom (the heart and the stomach) are closely related, and the two powers have their meeting place at the *solar plexus,* the great body brain that is located just behind the heart and the stomach.

The center of *power* is in the *throat,* at the *root of the tongue.* Here the disciple *Philip* is in charge.

Imagination is developed at a *point between the eyes* that is closely related to the *pituitary gland,* a small endocrine gland attached to the base of the brain which secretes hormones influencing body growth. The disciple who represents imagination is *Bartholomew,* also referred to as *Nathanael.*

At the *center front of the brain* is the seat of *understanding.* Understanding is also closely related to the *feet,* representing "the phase of the understanding that connects us with the outer or manifest world and reveals the right relationship toward worldly conditions in general" (*RW,* p. 74). *Thomas,* the disciple who liked to ask questions, represents understanding.

Just under the understanding, in the *center front of the brain,* is the place of the *will.* It is good to remember that the will is just below the understanding and should be always under the control and direction of the quality of understanding. *Matthew,* the tax collector, stands for the quality of will.

The *order* center is located just *behind the navel.* The faculty of order works through the *organs of digestion. James, the son of Alpheaus,* is the disciple who represents this power.

The *medulla oblongata, at the base of the brain in the back of the head,* is the home of *zeal,* or *enthusiasm.* Appropriately, this quality is represented by the Zealot in Jesus' group of twelve, *Simon the Cananaean.*

Renunciation, or *elimination,* works from a *nerve center at the base of the spinal column* and is closely allied with the *organs of elimination.* It is represented by Thaddaeus, sometimes called *Lebbaeus.*

The twelfth quality is *life,* which has its headquarters in the *generative organs,* at a point *back of the pubic bone. Judas,* the disciple who betrayed Jesus, represents life; but it must be remembered that after the resurrection, Judas was replaced by another disciple, *Matthias,* who stands for a higher realization of the life idea.

Although located in different parts of the body, the twelve powers are closely connected and should be developed as a harmonious whole. Under no circumstances should one faculty be developed to the exclusion of the others. Qualities or pairs of qualities are particularly closely related. They are to be unfolded together. And all powers are to be directed always by the Christ, from His throne in the top of the head.

As Jesus called the disciples and trained them to do his work, so we must call and train our faculties. We do this not in a personal way, but in a sense of identification with the Christ of our own being.

The centers in the body are awakened through positive, affirmative instruction, and the mind power is awakened at the same time and in the same way. Attention to a particular part of the body, the center of one of the powers, backed up by powerful prayer thought, will direct an energy flow to that sector and also will increase the conscious realization of that attribute in the mind.

Always remember in developing the twelve powers that under no circumstances can the qualities be forced to express themselves. They must be *invited.* These abilities actually rebel against force, which is a form of tension. They grow most easily in an atmosphere of relaxed expectancy, and they especially respond to happy, encouraging thoughts, and suggestions of praise and thanksgiving. Recognizing the living presence of God in our center and consciously blessing it is a vitalizing, energizing quality that contributes to the unfoldment of the attribute.

Development of your God-given potentiality is actually a matter of orderly growth. The qualities grow in your experience as they take their rightful place in your consciousness. As with all forms of nature, they grow best when nurtured and encouraged, but slow down when watched and measured.

Unfolding your twelve God-given faculties can be, and should be, a joyous experience, but it requires your thoughtful, dedicated desire and attention.

Remember, as you continue to invite the powers through the exercises given, that you are incorporating the spiritual body in the conscious, thinking part of your nature and in your physical body as well. You are becoming the "new creation" person and the "fourth dimension human." You are a forerunner of the new race of this new millennium. And the time, attention, and dedication that the job entails will pay off in ways you can neither imagine nor project at the present time.

Do not be timid about claiming and encouraging the development of your attributes. You are a God-designed, God-powered individual! Walk tall and speak boldly to your thoughts, feelings, and capabilities, and fully express your twelve spiritual powers.

Before we take up the first of the twelve faculties and the method for developing it, stop and declare silently to yourself: *Through the will and the work of the Father within, my twelve powers are developed and expressed—easily and in divine order.*

Speak them as the positive, powerful words they are, designed to awaken positive, powerful currents in your mind and body, but remember to encourage rather than try to force, to invite rather than push, to let the change in you come about easily and in divine order.

3

Awaken Your Faith Faculty

Of all the faculties, the one Jesus spoke of most frequently was faith. He was, in effect, saying to those who were with him and those of us who seek to follow, "Awaken your faith faculty!"

On numerous occasions he spoke positive, powerful words of faith, and those who were there to see the results marveled at the healings, the demonstrations of material supply, and even the apparent suspending of natural laws as he stilled the storm or walked on water, cooperating with laws not yet understood by his followers.

Always, when asked how it was done, Jesus spoke of faith. He said, "Your faith has made you well" (Mt. 9:22), or "According to your faith be it done to you" (Mt. 9:29). On one occasion he asked the disciples: "Why are you afraid? Have you no faith?" (Mk. 4:40). It was almost as though the faculty of faith was so strongly developed in him that he could not understand the lack of trust in others.

Have faith. Believe. Trust. Over and over, Jesus emphasized this first of our powers, and in one of his disciples, we watch the faculty develop.

Faith does not come all at once with a mighty thud. It must grow. It must be encouraged. It must be invited and then made welcome. As Simon, the crude fisherman, became Peter, the dedicated apostle, so the ability to trust God must grow in our lives.

Patience is necessary in developing all of our spiritual endowments, but it is particularly necessary in prompting the growth of our faith faculty. It is good to remember, if we fail to demonstrate our highest hopes and aims at a particular stage of our development, that Jesus never lost his temper with any of the disciples. He never became discouraged when Peter, the impulsive aspirant, failed to demonstrate completely. When the disciple, aglow with a greater conviction of God's power than he had ever had before, desired to walk on water, Jesus encouraged him. And when the same man, looking down, lost his ability to believe and started to sink, the Master reached out a hand and pulled him back.

So we, working from our own Christ, our own spiritual nature, must encourage and continue to develop our powers, refusing to condemn ourselves when we fail to live up to our greatest hopes and expectations. We, too, must continue to behold the potential, our God-given potential, in spite of limitations in our ability to express it fully at our present level of understanding.

Even when Peter denied him three times on the night before the crucifixion, Jesus did not condemn him for it. As Jesus continued to hold to his faith in the God faculties in Peter, the disciple continued to grow in faith until he was the channel for wonderful demonstrations of God-power—all through faith.

We, too, would develop this power. We, too, would learn to speak the word—the positive power word—that gets results. But in order to speak the word in this way, we must develop the inner conviction that makes the word effective. This is the faith that Jesus meant when he said, "All things are possible to him who believes" (Mk. 9:23).

Faith has been defined in many ways. The writer of Hebrews referred to it as "the assurance of things hoped for, the conviction of things not seen" (Heb. 11 :1). Understood in this light, faith is that quality in us which enables us to look past appearances of lack, limitation, or difficulty, to take hold of the divine idea and believe in it, even though we do not see any evidence of it except in our minds. Through faith we know with an inner knowing the Truth that has not yet expressed itself in our manifest world.

Charles Fillmore defines faith as "the perceiving power of the mind linked with the power to shape substance . . . a deep inner knowing that, that which is sought is already ours for the taking" (*RW,* p. 67). Here again we see that faith, exercised under the Christ dominion, is a faculty that actually brings about the good results we seek. It shapes substance according to the pattern we are holding in mind. It brings forth the good we have accepted with our perceptive inner vision. It is the connecting link between God-ideas in mind and the expression of them in the world.

Faith goes beyond thinking to knowing with the whole being the Truth of the unseen good.

The location of the faith center is significant. It is in the center of the head, between the ears and the eyes. When we put our faith in that which we see with our eyes or hear with our ears, we are using the faculty in a limited way and the results will come accordingly.

However, we can center the faculty of faith on our inner vision and our inner hearing, developing this faculty through prayer to know the potential God has given us. And when we do, our results will express the higher realization of our spiritual nature. At its highest level, faith is directed by our spiritual nature, from the Christ center at the crown of the head. We determine the direction of our faith, and as we do, we determine the results that we will have in our lives.

Conversely, when we look at the results we have been getting in our lives, we can see where we have been putting our faith. If the conditions are not what we want, we can, by changing the direction of our faith, change the results.

Peter—wavering, changeable Peter—who always wanted to believe, is the disciple who represents faith. And when we consider his name (which is the clue to his nature) and the change in his name, we begin to understand the way in which faith must be developed in us.

Peter was first known as Simon, which means "hearing." Had Peter not been willing to listen and learn, he would not have been able to stabilize his ability to believe in the unseen and, as an apostle, to call forth the positive, powerful results that are called "miracles."

As this disciple grew in his ability to believe, he became more receptive to inner guidance and direction—the "conviction of things not seen." Through his receptivity to knowledge of spiritual things, he was able to say to Jesus one day, "You are the Christ, the Son of the living God" (Mt. 16:16). Jesus, recognizing his growth, renamed Simon *Peter,* which means "rock." He went on to declare, "On this rock [the firm foundation of faith] I will build my church" (Mt. 16:18).

In developing the quality of faith, we must start as Peter did, by being receptive to Truth ideas and letting them grow in us until we can feel our absolute oneness with the quality of faith—feel in such a way that we no longer think in terms of having faith, but express it automatically, as Jesus did.

For the development of each of our twelve powers, we will have seven steps. We start with the acceptance of the concept in an intellectual way, develop it through increased understanding and prayer, and finally reach the place of spiritual identification or oneness with the power. These are the steps through which we develop faith:

1. Receptivity

In Romans 10:17, we are told, "Faith comes from what is heard, and what is heard comes by the preaching of Christ."

As Simon Peter started his spiritual development by listening and being receptive to the teachings of Jesus, so we start to develop our faith faculty by listening, learning, growing in understanding of spiritual truths, being receptive to God-ideas. Perhaps at first we find it difficult to believe that God is good and God is all. But by developing our ability to be receptive to Truth concepts, we take the first step in developing faith.

2. Assent

We take the step of assent by going beyond receptivity, to the point where we are willing to agree with the spiritual truths for the purpose of further, deeper investigation.

Assent says, "I'll think about it," or, "I'll try it." This is still a part of the intellectual development of our power of faith, but it is important. After we have listened and learned about God and His plan of good for our life, we must agree with it and go ahead under a premise that the spiritual truths we are learning have something to offer us.

If we do not determine those ideas to which we will be receptive and those concepts with which we will agree, we may find that, without realizing what we have done, we are believing and acting on concepts which we didn't choose—those false friends that may have sneaked in from the world through our physical eyes and ears.

3. Belief

Belief is the mental acknowledgment of Truth that comes as an outgrowth of the first two steps—an ability to believe intellectually, if not yet with the whole soul, the goodness of God and His desire to give good to us, His children.

At this point, we may say with the father who brought his son to Jesus, "I believe; help my unbelief!" (Mk. 9:24) Truth may seem wonderful to us, but as yet we are not able to step out on faith and put it to work in our lives.

This is all right. We should not condemn ourselves for failing to be able to trust God completely at this point. Peter went through a phase when he loved Jesus and believed intellectually what he taught, but would never have tried walking on the water.

4. Trust

Here we begin to make the great step from the intellectual acceptance of Truth ideas to the spiritual realization of them.

Charles Fillmore says of this step: "Trust is a cheaper brand of faith, but trust is better than mistrust. As a rule, people who merely trust in the Lord do not understand all the law. If they had understanding, they would affirm the presence and power of God until the very substance of Spirit would appear in consciousness—and this is faith established on a rock" (*TM,* p. 29). And this is what we do as we advance from this step to the next. We deepen our trust and reinforce it with understanding until we have a faith that is not simply passive, but active, a basis for action.

5. Faith

Here we begin to get results from our faith, turning our attention first to the pattern for perfection that was implanted in us in the beginning, the Christ, and believing in this divine potential with an understanding which inspires us to action.

Belief is good. Trust is better. But when we reach the step of faith, we are ready to act on what we believe. And we get results!

Of course, we may be like Peter at this point—acting on faith one minute and doubting the next. But if we continue to work, our faith grows as we use it. The law of use is the law of increase. Our faith is not yet perfect, but it has become a basis for action, "the power to do the seemingly impossible" (*RW,* p. 67).

6. Conviction

Conviction is "the divine assurance that comes to one when he is fully satisfied of the worth of Truth. Conviction refuses to be influenced by the senses because it is founded in spiritual thought" (*RW,* p. 44). Conviction is developed faith, settled and permanent. If it decides to walk on the water, it does not doubt and start to sink. It keeps on walking.

The word *conviction* is derived from two Latin words— *vincere,* meaning "to conquer," and *con,* which serves to intensify its meaning. When we have conquered all doubts, fears, and even the temptation to judge by our senses, we reach this point of spiritual conviction, the sixth step in the development of our faith faculty.

7. Realization

For each faculty, there is a step of conscious oneness, a point at which we no longer think in terms of developing or even using the power, but so identify with it in its spiritual entirety that we automatically act and react from faith perfected in oneness. We like to think that Peter came into the fullness of his faith faculty on the occasion of Pentecost, when the Apostles had their own spiritual awakening.

At this point of realization, we no longer *have* faith. We *are* the Christ expression of faith.

Instructions

To develop our faculty of faith from receptivity to realization, we speak to ourselves positive, powerful words of Truth.

You may want to start at the beginning and progress through each of the steps, as you build your power to believe. Or you may determine that you are ready for the second or third step, and start there. Wherever you are on the stairway of building faith, you can take with you (and live with it continually) the statement for the next step, building it into your consciousness until you feel that you have progressed to the next stage in building your faith faculty. It may take a year or years, or it may take a relatively short time for you to make that big step. You are the one who must determine the time it takes for you, because only you can look inside your own soul.

Remember, do not become tense and anxious about developing these God-given abilities. Invite them. Encourage them. Let them grow under the Christ dominion.

Remember, too, that the faith faculty is located in the center of the head, between the eyes and the ears. And as you speak these affirmations of Truth, aloud and silently, watch the senses to make sure they aid you in your spiritual growth. Always let your faith and your senses be ruled by the Christ of your own nature, spreading His light of Truth from the center at the apex of the head.

These are the statements for the steps:

Receptivity: *I am receptive to divine ideas.*
Assent: *I accept the idea of my innate divinity.*
Belief: *I believe with all my thinking ability that I am God's perfect child.*
Trust: *I trust God with all my heart.*
Faith: *I act on the faith that I am God's perfect child.*
Conviction: *I identify with the all-conquering Truth that I am a spiritual being, living in a spiritual universe, governed by spiritual ideas.*
Realization: *I am the Christ expression of faith.*

Faith is the first of your God-given powers. Encourage it. Let it grow in you, as you prepare to link it with your eleven other God-given faculties to develop the "fourth dimension" person you are designed to be.

God is blessing you now with faith!

Be

Strong

"The Lord has chosen you to build a house for the sanctuary; be strong, and do it" (1 Chron. 28:10). So King David exhorted his son Solomon to develop his God-given power of strength in order to build the temple, accomplishing his assigned task on earth.

The great king went on to point out to those who were assembled to hear his instructions: "Solomon my son, whom alone God has chosen, is young and inexperienced, and the work is great; for the palace will not be for man but for the Lord God" (1 Chron. 29:1). He then asked for volunteers to help Solomon in the great undertaking and blessed them with a prayer: "Thine, O Lord, is the greatness, and the power, and the glory, and the victory. . . . In thy hand are power and might; and in thy hand it is to make great and to give strength to all" (1 Chron. 29:11-12).

Strength was a faculty much prized by the leaders of the Hebrew people, and the Bible is full of exhortations to "be strong" and instructions to turn to God for that quality of strength. Strength is the second of the twelve powers that we are to awaken in mind and body as we develop our God-given potential. It is a power that is essential to the whole process of awakening our spiritual faculties, because without strength, we do not have the stamina necessary to follow through and unfold the other powers.

Many people think of the quality of strength as primarily a physical attribute, working through the human body. This is one aspect of strength, and a good one. Without physical strength, we may be limited in our ability to do God's work on earth. Of course we can, through spiritual methods, learn to develop physical strength.

However, strength is not simply a physical quality. As with all the twelve powers, it expresses itself on three levels, each one complementing the others in this life expression on the earth plane.

In the physical realm, strength is vitality, endurance, the ability to persist. In the mental area of expression, strength is that quality of mind which enables one to lead, to accomplish, to follow through on decisions, to establish purposes in life, and to hold firm to spiritual principles in daily living. It expresses itself as stability of character.

The highest expression, and the one that should determine the direction of strength in the other realms, is the spiritual realization of this quality. Here strength is closely allied with faith. In the symbology of the twelve disciples and the twelve qualities of mind that we are to develop as Jesus encouraged and developed his closest followers, strength and faith are represented by the brothers Andrew and Peter.

Peter must be the first of our qualities to be unfolded in a spiritual way, because without faith there is no impetus to action and no foundation for a program of spiritual growth. Faith also is our innate ability to see the unseen, plus the desire to persist in order to bring it forth. But faith has to be established in strength. The "two brothers" must grow together, both under the loving direction of our own Christ nature, the "perfect-human" idea within us. Faith must continually be strengthened, and strength must be inspired to right action by spiritual faith.

In a spiritual way, then, strength enables us to persist in prayer, to build a stronger and stronger faith in our spiritual nature and the activity of God through us, and to do the things that need to be done by us as a part of becoming the "fourth dimension" person that our twelve powers, spiritually developed, enable us to be.

The person who depends on physical strength alone is constantly being challenged by others in the human thought and eventually will be overcome by one who is stronger. This one will, in turn, be conquered by another who is yet stronger, and on it goes.

Mental strength alone meets a similar fate. Mental strength alone—pitted against the strong mind of another—may result in a test of wills, a human contest, with the same results. Only spiritual strength remains nonresistant, triumphant, regardless of the challenge. For the best results, both physical and mental strength must be rooted in the spiritual development of the strength faculty.

When David spoke to Solomon, telling him to "be strong," and when others in the Bible also gave this admonition, they were not pointing to strength as an end in itself. They were showing that this is an important quality which is necessary if we are to do the work God has for us to do, but a quality which is to be used by us. Under no circumstances should developing strength of body or mind be our only goal of existence. Strength is made to serve us and to serve us *best* in the evolutionary process of developing the God-ideated human of the future.

Always keep Andrew, your faculty of strength, under the direction of the Christ, and never separate yourself from your divine Source by misusing this power or by feeling that you, in your human self, are sufficient in your own strength.

Strength is a gift of God. As with all God's gifts, it flows most easily and freely when it is invited, made welcome, and appreciated as a spiritual endowment. You are always strongest when you are most faithful in maintaining a close connection with God.

Andrew was a fisherman when he first met Jesus. He had to be strong physically to do the hard work of handling the heavy nets of fish. As he followed Jesus, though, he had to develop strength in another way: as the ability to determine a course of action and persist in it. Finally, he had to follow through all the way in his spiritual growth, along with his brother Peter.

It is easy today for us to think that we would have followed Jesus gladly, willingly leaving everything else behind, even continuing his work after the crucifixion and Resurrection, under difficulties that were not only mental but even entailed physical suffering. But would we?

Andrew the disciple had a special kind of strength. Strength is a quality that we can and must develop if we are to bring forth our God-given potential. It is to be brought forth along with the other eleven powers, but it must be basic in our growth.

As you begin your development of this faculty represented by Andrew, declare quietly to yourself: *Through the will and the work of the Father within, my God-given potential of strength is developed and expressed—easily and in divine order.* Remember that strength is to be developed easily, not with tension and strain, but with a relaxed, trusting attitude.

The center of strength is in the small of the back. It is here that we place our attention as we hold to the faith in God as our strength. The ganglionic center that represents strength is closely allied with the adrenals, the glands which are sometimes referred to as the "fighters of the body." These glands are designed to serve the human body in a very special way. They secrete adrenaline, a substance that flows into the body and immediately stimulates increased vitality to do whatever needs to be done.

In earlier times, the adrenals served the purpose of enabling humans to perform great physical feats, such as were necessary to our physical survival in the world. Today, individuals often awaken these glands with some call for increased physical strength. However, those who misuse this God-given secretion by mentally fighting or resisting their environment or other persons find that the strength they have received in the form of adrenaline, misused, is a poison to the body. The God-given powers are to be God-directed and used only for good. The centers in the body are to be treated as centers of spiritual light, directed always by the Christ.

Strength is not to be sought as an end in itself, but it is to be respected. Misuse of the strength God gives will cause a feeling of depletion and weakness. As we develop strength, we must learn to exercise control over wasting this precious quality in such activities as emotional outbursts of anger or despair or frustration, all of which rob us and leave us more susceptible to negative suggestions in mind and body.

Strength is our right as a child of God. We do not inherit weakness. We do not have to accept anything less than a perfect expression of physical, mental, and spiritual strength. But we must pay the price of learning to watch and train our thoughts and feelings as we develop the vitality and endurance that is our divine inheritance.

As with all the powers, strength is consciously awakened first in the intellectual nature and then developed (through prayerful concentration on the idea) to be a spiritual realization of oneness with the Source of all strength. The result is a continuous, limitless supply of all that this quality means. It is accomplished under the direction of the Christ, or God Self.

These are the steps through which we develop strength:

I. Nonresistance

In order to develop the quality of strength, we must begin by getting rid of habits that continually deplete this faculty. Resistance is the greatest theft of strength. Through anger, fear, argument, and other forms of resistance—even the mental tendency to worry—we have tirades of mind and emotions that leave us feeling depleted and weak. There is no point in trying to develop the attribute of strength if we are, at the same time, continually dissipating this power through mental and emotional orgies of negation. Control and self-discipline are parts of developing all the faculties that make us the tremendous creations we are, and they are particularly important in the development of strength. You resist when you forcefully try to convert others to your opinion. You resist when you actively oppose another's attempt to convert you. You resist when you lose your temper, worry about things, and generally try to fight—mentally, emotionally, or physically.

Nonresistance is not a negative quality. It does not require that you let others take advantage of you. It simply asks that you control your own thinking and feeling in such a way that you can cope with life without becoming involved in a resistant attitude which gives power to wrong. This is the first step in building strength.

2. Relaxation

More can be accomplished in a feeling of relaxation than in an attitude of forcing and pushing. Once you have freed yourself from mental and emotional habits of resistance, you can learn the art of relaxation, the relaxation that enables you to work and play without tension and strain.

Psychologists proved with time and motion studies years ago that taking an occasional break from a demanding task will enable one to accomplish more in less time. This is one method of relaxation that will increase your strength and help you to use it to better advantage.

Athletes, who depend on their physical strength to accomplish their purpose, are also learning the importance of mental attitudes. The greatest athletes have learned to increase their endurance through practiced relaxation of mind and body, even as they compete.

Relaxation may not be easy for one who has lived and worked under tension over a long period of time, but it can be learned. Do it in specific times of speaking to the various parts of your body and telling them to relax. Speak to your mind and command it (in a relaxed way) to release tense thoughts and attitudes. Remind yourself during the day, as you find yourself tightening up, to "relax and let go." If a job becomes burdensome and difficult, take a relaxation break and return to it refreshed. As you practice these simple methods, you will be moving up the ascending scale of increased strength. Again, this step requires control and self-discipline, but it pays tremendous dividends!

3. Infilling

Now we are ready to begin receiving the gift of strength from God. It is not until we have freed ourselves from the destructive habits of resistance and learned the art of relaxation that we are able to be a clear channel for the inflow of increased strength.

As we come to the step of infilling, we make it a point, in our regular prayer time, simply to open ourselves to God for the inflow of His strength as a spiritual gift. This is never in a sense of straining to receive, but rather in the attitude of opening to the outpouring of vital life through our whole being.

4. Direction

As you begin to receive increased strength from God, remember that you are responsible for using the gifts of God wisely. Used for good, they will increase, but dissipated unwisely, they will decrease.

So, good management becomes an important step. You must guide the strength you are receiving from God into channels of good, using it always under His direction. Sometimes when people begin to receive answers to prayer and see an increase in their good, they become carried away with the good things that have happened and forget the Source from which the blessings came.

As you feel your strength increasing, make it a practice to use it always under God's guidance. Remember, your purpose here on earth is to fulfill God's plan of good and the powers are given to you to use in accomplishing this end.

5. Incorporation

Here we begin to embody strength in various ways—in our physical bodies as vitality and vigor; in our minds as increased stability of purpose and decision; and in our spiritual lives as increased activity of persistence in prayer, strengthened faith, and an ability to stand tall in our spiritual natures.

Strength is not simply something we talk about or draw on at certain times; it becomes a part of our makeups, incorporated into our very beings, in all phases of their expression.

Sometimes pictures of Jesus Christ show him as a weak man, a man burdened by sorrows. Nothing could be further from the true picture of our Way-Shower. Jesus started life as a carpenter, in an activity that required a strong back and capable hands. He had to be strong to be the builder of houses, the contractor, that a carpenter was in those days. Even as a boy he "increased in wisdom and in stature, and in favor with God and man" (Lk. 2:52).

Jesus, through spiritual methods, incorporated ideas of strength into his mind and body and built an ability to cope with life above and beyond anything we normally see in any other person. And Jesus said, "Follow me."

6. Strength

After we have learned to receive strength from God and incorporate this attribute into our minds, bodies, and spiritual natures, we know ourselves as strong. We feel strength as a living quality working in and through us.

We are free from weakness, in all three phases of living. We find it easy to stand firm in our purpose and direction. We have an impetus to do right things and an ability to accomplish unlimited good. We are strong!

7. Supremacy

Supremacy is the "supreme strength as demonstrated by Jesus . . . attained by one who trusts in Spirit" (*TM,* p. 37). Here we no longer think in terms of being strong or having strength. The supreme idea of strength is so incorporated into the whole being that it flows through us as the perfect ability to receive and use strength from God to fill every need without conscious volition. The one who reaches this place is in the stream of cosmic strength; it pours in and through one's life to vitalize every department of life and living.

Jesus maintained his supremacy by continuing to withdraw from the crowds for times of receiving from God in prayer, thus maintaining his conscious connection with Spirit at the highest level.

Instructions

Start at the beginning and develop your strength through the methods given for each degree; or if you feel that you have progressed to a certain point, start on that step in developing strength. Dedicate yourself to it and hold in mind the suggestions given for self-discipline and control and also the affirmative statement for that stage. Don't rush. Let strength grow in you through your own realization of it in all departments of your being.

The strength center is in the small of the back. Place your attention at this ganglionic center as you use positive, powerful words of strength. Expect a response of strength in all phases of your life, but do not try to check up on it. Just let it grow, always under the direction of the Christ, your own spiritual nature, from its ruling point at the top of the head.

The affirmative statements for developing the strength faculty follow.

> Nonresistance: *Nothing has any power to make me resistant or resentful. I stand firm in God.*
>
> Relaxation: *I am relaxed—mentally, physically, and spiritually.*
>
> Infilling: *Let the strength of God now flow into my mind and body.*
>
> Direction: *My strength grows daily as I follow God's direction in its right use.*
>
> Incorporation: *I incorporate ideas of God's strength into all I think, feel, say, and do—all day long.*
>
> Strength: *I am strong in the Lord.*
>
> Supremacy: *I am one with infinite strength.*

Strength is your God-given right. Let it grow in conjunction with its brother, faith, as you develop your God-given potentiality, always under the guidance of your own spiritual nature, the Christ within.

5

Let
Your
Light
Shine

One of the faculties most prized by Jesus was the gift of wisdom, or spiritual judgment.

Frequently he pointed to correct methods of judgment. He said:

"Do not judge by appearances, but judge with right judgment" (Jn. 7:24).

"You judge according to the flesh, I judge no one. Yet even if I do judge, my judgment is true, for it is not I alone that judge, but I and he who sent me" (Jn. 8:15-16).

"Judge not, that you be not judged. For with the judgment you pronounce you will be judged . . ." (Mt. 7:1-2).

Always he pointed to the importance of judging by the standards of the higher Self, rather than by the example set in the world. Never did he react to any person or any situation with the expected response of human living, but always he acted and spoke from the light within himself, the light that enabled him to judge by spiritual methods, to answer from divine insight into the motives of others, the potentiality of good and the revelation of the Christ within.

His judgment and his wisdom went far beyond the perception, knowledge, and judgment of even the most learned men of the day, because his faculty of knowing was developed by a conscious acquaintance with the Source and a desire to express the wisdom of Spirit. He never drew conclusions simply from intellectual knowledge.

As we follow Jesus in developing our God-given potential, we, too, must learn to "judge with right judgment" and to turn to the inner spiritual knowing. We cannot afford to allow ourselves to be caught up in judging according to appearances, making decisions based simply on intellectual knowledge, or accepting limiting concepts constantly presented to us by the worldly viewpoint. Jesus learned to judge by right judgment, and so can we, if we will consciously and conscientiously develop our faculty of wisdom and spiritual judgment.

The ganglionic center that is associated with the faculty of wisdom is located in the pit of the stomach and is closely allied with the solar plexus, the area behind the heart and stomach which is sometimes referred to as the "body brain." As with all the powers, wisdom functions in all three phases of man's being. This power of judgment or discrimination works through the physical, the mental, and also the spiritual nature. It works according to the way in which the individual directs its activity.

Human judgment may be based on criticism, condemnation, and fearfulness, and it will express itself in both the physical body and the thinking ability as a kind of poison. Unloving, critical thoughts react particularly on the wisdom center at the pit of the stomach and may result in such ailments as ulcers, indigestion, or other difficulties of the stomach area and heart.

On the other hand, when we learn to exercise the faculty of judgment in the inner illumination by Spirit, we will automatically be expressing a greater degree of physical health. This applies particularly to the digestion and other phases of health connected with the stomach area.

Referring to the wisdom center at the pit of the stomach and the solar plexus area behind the stomach, Charles Fillmore explains: "The presiding intelligence at this center knows what is going on, especially in the domain of consciousness pertaining to the body and its needs. Chemistry is its specialty; it also knows all that pertains to the sensations of soul and body. In its highest phase it makes union with the white light of Spirit functioning in the top brain" (*TM,* p. 49).

Here we are reminded that the Christ idea, the God Self within us, is directly connected to all the powers through their centers in the body and that the best results are obtained by allowing the Christ to direct the physical, mental, and spiritual development of all the faculties.

As you unfold the various attributes, continue to picture the white light of Spirit coming down from the top of the head to awaken, guide, and direct the development of each center. As Jesus awakened, guided, and directed the potentialities in the twelve disciples, so the Christ of us, our higher nature, must be put in charge of the development of our powers.

While it is important to remember that we are to develop all the twelve powers, there are certain powers which are most closely allied with the Christ in this development. One of these is the faculty of wisdom, or judgment, represented by James, the son of Zebedee.

The three disciples who were with Jesus on particularly significant occasions in his life were Peter, representing faith, and the brothers James and John, standing for wisdom and love. When Jesus went into the house to raise Jairus' daughter from the dead, he took with him Peter, James, and John. These three were also with him on the Mount of Transfiguration, when he was transformed and appeared to them in the radiant light of his spiritual body. They went with him even into the garden of Gethsemane, where he asked them to wait and watch with him while he prayed.

So faith, wisdom, and love must be brought into everything we do. These three faculties are to be developed together, and wisdom and love, the two brothers, are actually complementary to each other. Wisdom without love is cold. But love without wisdom is misguided and impetuous.

James and John, wisdom and love, preside in adjoining areas of the body, wisdom in the pit of the stomach and love in the heart. They come together in the great solar nerve center, the solar plexus at the back of the heart and the stomach. Here they earn their nickname, "sons of thunder," as they have a tremendous vibratory effect on the whole body. Fillmore explains, "All fervor, all the high energy that comes from soul, passes through these centers" (*TM,* p. 20).

Wisdom, the highest form of spiritual knowing, includes divine judgment, discrimination, intuition, and other activities of mind that come under the heading of pure knowing. Wisdom is not dependent on reasoning, intellectual understanding, or deduction. It simply shines as the light from within that illumines the way and reveals whatever needs to be shown at a particular time. It is "the voice of God within . . . mental action based on the Christ Truth within" (*RW,* p. 211).

Our purpose in developing this faculty is to let the light of Spirit shine through us, directing all our thoughts, words, actions, and motivations. Wisdom must also be employed in directing the activities and unfoldment of the other eleven qualities.

While the ultimate expression of the faculty is in the form of the clear, white inner light of knowing, its development begins in us as a process of re-education of our ability to know. Had we always maintained a clear, beautiful connection with Spirit through the Christ Mind, our faculty of wisdom would be pouring out to us a constant, limitless stream of divine insight and guidance. But because we have chosen to clutter our thinking with false concepts, the world's standards, and other limiting forms of intellectual evaluation we must re-educate our faculty of discrimination and judgment in order to awaken the spiritual light of knowing within us.

These are the steps through which we develop our wisdom faculty, starting with a process of intellectual training and building, through the enlightenment of mind and body, to the point where we are so completely identified with the spiritual-being idea that we know as Jesus knew:

1. Unlearning

In the development of several different faculties, we find that we must first correct wrong habits of thinking in order to provide a clear channel through which the power can flow. In seeking the clear, white light of inner knowing, we must cleanse the outlet of wrong concepts and attitudes in order to keep from adulterating the true knowledge as it comes through. If we filter the God-ideas through our human preconceptions and limitations, we find that our knowledge is distorted and unclear. It is only as we are clear channels that our power of intuitive knowing is functioning at maximum efficiency.

So we must unlearn. We must clear our minds of all false ideas of lack and limitation, fear, intolerance, disease, and difficulty. We must even cure ourselves of the habit of saying, "I don't know," as we grow into the understanding that there is a Spirit in us which knows whatever we need to know. This is the channel that is opened as we retrain our thinking ability and move into the area of spiritual intuition—the immediate receiving of whatever knowledge we need at the time.

Fillmore explains, "We find that at every upward step we take in our evolution there is a sloughing off of, a doing away with, some parts of consciousness that do not accord with the higher principles" (*ASP*, p. 154). In the development of wisdom, this step is unlearning.

2. Learning

Nature abhors a vacuum. We must replace the old concepts we are unlearning with new spiritual truths. Therefore, these first two steps in developing the faculty of wisdom and spiritual judgment must be employed simultaneously.

As we teach ourselves, "There is nothing to fear," for instance, we must follow up with the thought "The protecting presence of God guards and guides me all day long." It is a procedure involving total re-education of our thinking processes, so that we consciously reject the thoughts which do not belong to us in our spiritual nature and, at the same time, lay hold of the truths which will help us to become acquainted with another way of thinking. It is not enough to release; we must also refill.

We learn Truth principles from teachers, writers, ministers, and other channels for God-ideas. It is good for us to study and learn. But we must do more than simply read or listen. We must begin to incorporate the new habits of thinking into everything we entertain in our minds all day long, so that we automatically reject a negative suggestion which may be presented and replace it with the proper Truth idea we are learning. This is still on the intellectual level, but it is an important part of mind training.

3. Acknowledgment

As an extension of the learning process, we advance to the step of acknowledgment. *To learn* means "to get knowledge of (a subject) . . . by study or experience . . . to memorize . . . to acquire as a habit or attitude." *To acknowledge* means "to admit to be true."

A child may learn something in school, so that he has knowledge of it. He may be able to recite it by rote but he may have no feeling for it or understanding of it.

Acknowledgment is the step through which we mentally accept what we have learned. As we begin consciously to receive these new spiritual ideas in mind, we grow in our ability to work with them and we see the familiar people and situations in our world in a new light.

Here we must avoid the tendency to judge with human judgment, based on our intellectual perception—even though we may be sure we are correct. Some who have studied these ideas for a while and are accepting them from an intellectual viewpoint have a tendency to judge the errors of others too harshly.

Jesus warned against this human judgment. God does not condemn, and neither should we. Whenever we find our understanding of Truth leading us to condemnation, we must remind ourselves, "Judge not, that you be not judged." Increased knowledge is given to us for use in improving our own lives, and as we grow in the development of this faculty, we will come to the point of seeing only the Christ in others, not the faults.

So we acknowledge the truths we are learning in order to increase our ability to apply them in our lives.

4. Reason

The more we work with ideas, the more they reveal other facets to us. In a negative way, we see this in the process of worry. By revolving various negative possibilities in our mind, we can produce other negative possibilities and greater reasons for worry and apprehension.

On the positive side, by letting basic Truth ideas work in mind we begin to come up with new understanding and application of these principles. For instance, we may take two known items—for example, "God is all good" and "I am God's child and inherit from Him"—and come up with the new idea "If I am God's child and inherit what He is, then I, too, am good." This can be a tremendous revelation to one who has been taught that he is a miserable sinner or something of the sort. This is the point in the development of wisdom when we move beyond the intellectual acceptance of Truth ideas into the place where we begin to come up with new ideas or combinations of thoughts that lead us into a depth of knowledge we never had before.

Reason may be employed as an intellectual process, but it also becomes the bridge to the spiritual development of the faculty of wisdom, because it leads us into a higher, expanded field of knowledge, where new concepts come forth as the result of our contemplation and logical thought about what we have already learned and accepted mentally. Meditation, one of the steps in prayer, is a form of development of the reasoning ability as a part of our forward spiritual motion.

5. Insight

At last we come to the point where we begin to receive flashes of spiritual knowing. We still may not be completely in tune with the Source, but we do have experiences of discerning something beyond what we know in an intellectual way. At this point, we may be receiving guidance from time to time, somehow knowing what we should do in a certain situation.

Unlearning, learning, and acknowledgment are all important in our intellectual development of knowledge. Reason serves as a bridge that we cross along the way. But it is when we are no longer feverishly searching that we begin to have—in a calm, peaceful frame of mind—this inner sight, this insight which may be unsubstantial and fleeting, but which is the beginning of our awakening to a clear, white light of spiritual knowing that burns in us brightly at all times.

6. Wisdom

Here insight becomes full-grown. It is no longer an occasional flash of inner knowing, but an inner flame of light that enables us to know immediately and judge constantly—not as the world knows or judges, but from the Christ within. This is the power of wisdom and spiritual judgment that Jesus demonstrated so beautifully.

Fillmore explains: "When we awaken to the reality of our being, the light begins to break upon us from within and we know the truth. . . . When this quickening occurs, we find ourself discriminating between the good and the evil. We no longer accept the race standards or the teachings of the worldly wise, but we 'judge righteous judgment'; we know with an inner intuition, and we judge men and events from a new viewpoint" (*TM*, p. 44). We have the fully developed faculty of wisdom.

7. Knowing

Now we no longer *have* wisdom. We *are* wisdom. Through a pure and perfect connection with Spirit, we live in the light continually. We do not have to ask and receive an answer. We are not conscious of having wisdom at all. We *know.* We think and act continually from the Spirit of knowing within us.

On the level of insight, we have glimpses of wisdom. On the next level of wisdom, we live with the light and draw from it. But on the highest level of the development of this faculty, we are one with divine knowledge. It is so completely developed in us that we no longer have to think about it at all. We are able to say and know, "I and the Father are one" (Jn. 10:30).

Jesus promised, "I am the light of the world; he who follows me will not walk in darkness, but will have the light of life" (Jn. 8:1-2). At this point we do not just have the light shining within us, we *are* that light—and we know it.

Instructions

To develop your faculty of wisdom, advance step-by-step up the ladder by spending time and concentrated thought on each part of the progression. Remember that unlearning should be linked with learning in the process. Remind yourself from time to time to become relaxed and receptive to the Spirit within you that knows. Perhaps you will begin to receive those flashes of insight sooner than you expect.

The wisdom center is in the pit of the stomach, and it is linked with love at the solar plexus. Keep your attention at this point as you develop your ability to know.

The following statements are not simply words. They are ideas, designed to help you to know what you need to know at a particular time in your development of this power. Use them wisely, letting them awaken greater powers of knowing in you as you move up step-by-step.

> Unlearning: *I joyously release false concepts of the past.*
> Learning: *I conscientiously learn the Truth about God and me.*
> Acknowledgment: *I wholeheartedly acknowledge and accept new ideas of Truth.*
> Reason: *I enthusiastically expand my knowledge of the basic principles of Truth.*
> Insight: *I see past appearances to the Truth.*
> Wisdom: *Through the light of the Christ in me, I know the Truth.*
> Knowing: *I am one with the all-knowing Mind of God.*

Remember, as you develop wisdom, that this center is closely linked to the Christ and that as you concentrate on opening the way, all the knowing of Spirit pours in to light your whole being. Wisdom will guide you in your development of the other eleven powers.

6

Let
There
Be
Love

Everybody loves somebody or something—sometime, somewhere, somehow. It may seem to be only one's self or one's problems—or maybe one's rigid opinions. But love must play a part in the life of every individual. It is our nature to love.

Love is the most universally recognized and most frequently misinterpreted of the twelve powers. It is a part of life and living, and without love, people perish. Even a wrong interpretation of this attribute of God is better than no love at all. But, as those who are seeking to unfold all the faculties under God direction, we can be guided into the right use and development of this power. As we let the divine interpretation of love unfold in our lives, we will find that it opens the door to experiences of God's good, above and beyond anything we have ever thought was possible.

In Spirit, love is "the pure essence of Being that binds together the whole human family" (*RW,* p. 124). It is the harmonizing, healing, unifying, attracting power in the universe. In nature, it works as gravity. In Divine Mind, it is the idea of universal harmony and unity, that which binds together the whole of God's creation into one harmonious unit so that even the tiniest movement of a person's finger displaces atoms out in space; and the thoughts and feelings of our civilization combine to form a race consciousness which determines the future of all humankind. We are indissolubly linked with everything in God's creation, and the only place we can ever be separate from it is in our own thinking-feeling nature.

When Jesus prayed the prayer of at-one-ment with his disciples, as reported so beautifully by John, the love disciple, he was calling attention to the ultimate activity of love, the spiritual oneness that pervades everything in the universe.

Love and its ultimate expression of oneness operate on three levels. On the physical level, love can be seen as the link between atom and atom, the energy that holds together the forms of matter we see. It operates as the attracting power of gravity that magnetizes earth forms to the earth.

As we look out into the universe, we see it in the universal harmony that makes a divine pattern of stars and planets, galaxies, and other worlds beyond our present knowledge, each in its right place in relation to all the others and each having its own particular effect upon the whole. No one exists to himself, any more than any part of the universe can cut itself off from any other part. Only in our minds can we feel ourselves alone. Only in our thinking-feeling nature can we deny the love principle.

Love *is.* Love continues to be, just as the sun continues to shine, whether or not we know it is there, whether or not we can see it, whether or not we believe in it.

On the level of mind, in the human plane, love (or oneness, a sense of identification) is the power that draws people together as families and friends. Also in mind, at a higher level of development, it can be the inner light that enables us to see good in all persons, to identify with the higher nature of other individuals, even when they fail to express it.

As Charles Fillmore explains it: "Love is an inner quality that sees good everywhere and in everybody. It insists that all is good, and by refusing to see anything but good it causes that quality finally to appear uppermost in itself, and in all things" (*RW,* p. 125). This is a mental application of the idea of love. However, unwisely applied, it may cause difficulties and limitations. For instance, one who loves another person in a human way may be so blind to the other's faults as to be willing to fight the world for the other person, regardless of the wrongs that person perpetrates. Any time love, or our understanding of it, leads us to fight, we should take a second look at the *way* we are loving. The right application of the power will result in a warm, comfortable feeling that enables us to see the good in all persons, not just in those with whom we have close personal relationships.

This right mental approach leads naturally to the spiritual development of the faculty as an experience of oneness that recognizes God in and through every part of the universe. In the complete realization of the love idea, we not only recognize but also feel our unseen link with the good in all persons and even in all forms of life in our universe, seen and unseen.

The love center in the body is in the heart. As the heart circulates life-giving blood throughout the body, so a right concept of love circulates life-giving sustenance through our thinking-feeling nature, as well as through our body and affairs. Development of the God-consciousness of oneness enriches all phases of the life it enters. The faculties of love, centered in the heart, and wisdom, from its seat at the pit of the stomach, meet in the solar plexus, at the back of the heart and stomach.

In considering the unfoldment of the love faculty, we must make sure that we link it always with wisdom and that we build both attributes always under the direction of the Christ. As Jesus encouraged and developed the disciples, so we must encourage and develop the faculties they represent, always remembering to keep the Christ, our own God nature, in charge.

Wisdom and love are represented by the two brothers, James and John, sons of Zebedee. John, who, tradition tells us, wrote the fourth gospel, spoke of himself as "the disciple whom he [Jesus] loved" (Jn. 19:26). So it is only natural that John should be associated with the idea of love. He was the disciple who demonstrated possibly the greatest love for the Master Teacher, for he was able to receive the tremendous revelation of the Jesus Christ message and its prophecy for the future.

So John represents love; but we find that James was with John and Jesus on several great occasions reported in The Gospels. Both qualities are essential to the production of any great idea. Wisdom and love are not only two of the twelve faculties of man, but they are also the two phases of God that combine to produce creative activity of any kind.

Love without wisdom has a tendency to be blind, easily misled, foolish in its actions. On the other hand, wisdom without love may be harsh and cold, unfeeling in its activity. Linked in the Mind of God, working from pure knowing and the ultimate oneness, they produce perfect ideas in mind and manifestation.

It is well for us to remember that the creative activity of God is based in the two phases—Father-Mother, male-female, wisdom-love—because it is through the right use of these two powers that we are able to produce divinely inspired ideas, and from them, perfect results in our manifest world.

Fillmore explains: "Divine Mind blessed the union of wisdom and love and pronounced on them the increase of Spirit. When wisdom and love are unified in the individual consciousness, man is a master of ideas and brings forth under the original creative law" (*MG,* p. 27).

This is the way in which we would have love and wisdom working for us in consciousness, always under God direction, producing perfect results in our lives.

However, in linking love with wisdom, we must not take anything away from this feminine-mother quality. It is love that looks past appearances to behold the Truth of being. It is love that enables us to live in harmony with all our universe. It is love that heals, prospers, attracts, holds, and makes real the good ideas. And divine love is the greatest power for protection in the universe.

Jesus had great love and respect for the disciple John. It was to this disciple that he, speaking from the cross, committed the care of his mother. As the eldest son, it was his responsibility to provide for his mother. At the Lord's Supper, we are told that John was the one who was "lying close to the breast of Jesus" (Jn. 13:23).

Without love in its physical application, established through gravity and the right relationship between stars and galaxies in space, it would seem that our universe would literally fall apart. And without the God-directed expression of love in our lives, we will find that the whole experience seems meaningless and futile. Love gives body to our aspirations and direction to our evolution.

It is not necessary for us to like all that we see in our world. We do not have to agree with the wrong things that people do. But regardless of appearances, we must love the Christ or God in all persons and all things. We must, because it is our nature to love and because "he first loved us."

Love becomes a quality that takes over and permeates our thinking-feeling nature, but it begins as an idea in mind. As with the other powers, we learn to develop the faculty of love first through an intellectual approach; then we let it build to the point where it becomes a spiritual experience and finally a realization of oneness with the idea in Divine Mind.

The steps for developing love are as follows:

1. Interest

The love idea is awakened in intellectual persons through interest. You can never love anyone or anything that does not first interest you. Love between a boy and a girl begins with interest. Love in family relationships must involve interest. Love for work or new ideas or anything in the way of worthwhile achievement always begins as interest.

Interest is defined by Webster as "a feeling of intentness, concern, or curiosity about something" and also as "a share in something; anything in which one participates or has a share."

Interest in anything actually gives us a share in the thing that interests us, even if it is only a feeling of being a part of it (in a way, this is a sense of oneness). Interest in a baseball game makes one a part of the game. Interest in what the neighbors are doing may make a lonely person feel more a part of life.

Of course, as applied here, we want to give our interest to God and to finding God in our world, seeking out the good in all persons and situations, becoming more interested in the divine potential than in the limitations of ourselves or others. In developing love through this first step, we must learn to literally become interested in good, and the more we become interested in good, the more we have a share in it.

2. Acquaintance

Acquaintance naturally follows interest, though there is some overlapping in these steps. When we are interested in something, we want to become better acquainted with it. As we develop our interest in searching out the good and having a share in it, we naturally seek a close acquaintance, "knowledge (of something or someone) got from personal experience or contact" with the Source of good.

Our personal experience of God comes first from looking for evidence of His good around and about. Then our increased interest must lead us to a deeper search for personal knowledge of Spirit through prayer. This is an early movement along the pathway of the development of love.

3. Affection

In a human love relationship, there is first the interest, then the acquaintance, which leads to a feeling of affection. Affection is the budding idea of love that survives closer acquaintance with the person, job, or thing which first arouses interest.

In the development of the love idea as a spiritual attribute in consciousness, affection is the warm feeling which begins to grow in us, an awakening, a fondness which picks us up and starts us across the bridge of spiritual awakening to the point where we have such a good feeling about God (not just an intellectual understanding, but a warm liking) that we want to know more; we want to experience a greater realization of His love. That leads naturally to the next step across the bridge to the spiritual realization of the love idea.

4. Attraction

Here the love power itself takes hold and begins to carry us forward. We are caught up in something that is working through us as a magnet, drawing us deeper and ever deeper into the mysterious activity of love. We can't stop. We are attracted or impelled into knowing more of the Truth of our being, coming closer to God in consciousness, feeling a greater realization of our oneness with the great allness of Spirit.

When we let it take over in our lives and transform us from within, the magnetic power of love is stronger than any force in the universe. We begin to see all things in a new light. As people "in love" begin to discover new beauty and new greatness in each other, so we, through the attracting, energizing spirit of love awakening in us, begin to see ourselves and our world in a new light. Inspired by our new vision, we are aroused to greater spiritual activity. We deeply desire to know more, to feel more, to enter fully into the spiritual adventure of loving and living.

Here we must be sure that we are linking love with wisdom, because if we follow love alone, we may make unwise decisions or be carried away by a burst of "love power" without proper direction. But love and wisdom, working together, literally carry us forward into the greatest spiritual adventure of our lives.

5. Love

When we reach this point, we are so in tune with God's love that we are seeing good everywhere, even in appearances which seem to deny it. We are able to experience the love feeling in such a way that we know the potential in all persons, even when they themselves are refusing to express it.

We are in spiritual harmony with the love idea and are seeing our world in a whole new light. Love no longer differentiates, loving just one person to the exclusion of all others. It bathes all in a warm glow that lightens the heart and illumines the facial expression with warmth and light. Love radiates, attracts, heals, and harmonizes—love *is.*

6. Identification

In human relationships, love leads to a desire for a closer sense of identification. This may result in marriage or in planned activities designed to hold a family together or in organizations of people who are interested in the same loved ideals or goals.

In the spiritual unfoldment of love power, the step of identification is a point beyond just loving God and loving good. It is that place where we feel ourselves a part of God. There is a particular closeness that makes us able to realize "I am a child of God" and to know ourselves as a part of God's family, identified with Him in such a way that we have a desire for an even stronger, deeper bond, something which will link us indissolubly and irrevocably with God in all things, at all times, in all ways. And that brings us to the ultimate realization of our oneness.

7. At-one-ment

One of the most beautiful prayers in the Bible is given in John 17. Some call it the prayer of atonement. In Unity, we refer to it as the prayer of at-one-ment, the meditation in which Jesus revealed to the disciples his realization of oneness with

God, with them, and with all who were to follow—the ultimate realization of divine unity.

As we seek to take this last step up the ladder of love, we will want to refer often to these words of Jesus and to consider what the Way-Shower meant when he prayed, "I in them and you in me, that they may become completely one" (Jn. 17:23 NRSV). These are not words to be considered coldly or critically, but ideas we must allow to unfold in us when we have reached the point of feeling the warmth of God's love flowing through us in such a way that our greatest desire is to express it, to identify with it, to *be* it. This is the ultimate fulfillment of the love idea.

Instructions

Decide where you are in the development of your divine endowment of love, or start at the beginning by building your interest in God and in good so strongly that you then are ready to move on to the next step and the next. Love is not a power that you can consider from a strictly intellectual viewpoint, but it can be awakened by conscious mental attention to the idea. Decide where you are ready to work, and then use the following statements to help you progress in developing your God-given ability to love.

Interest: *Enthusiastically I seek to learn more about God.*
Acquaintance: *I seek out God in all persons, places, and circumstances.*

Affection: *A warm and happy feeling toward God is growing in my heart.*

Attraction: *Through the power of divine attraction, I am
drawn ever closer to God.*

Love: *I let God's love flow through me every moment of
every day.*

Identification: *I look with God's eyes of love.*

At-one-ment: *I am one with God, and God is perfect
love.*

As you choose your love attitude, let it develop in conjunction with its brother, wisdom. Continue to use your prayer
thought for developing the wisdom and judgment faculty, following it with the love realization. Center your attention on
the solar plexus, the great nerve center of your being, as you
awaken these two powers, the "sons of thunder." Let them
grow, but keep them always under the direction of the Christ,
spreading the light of perfect direction from the center at the
top of the head.

Open
the
Power
Channel

Power! The word itself has a magical, mystical sound. Through the years the idea of power has been the main goal of existence in more than one person's life—the never-ending search for power over other people, power in the political or ecclesiastical area, power to accomplish miracles, power to amaze and mystify others. Power, power, power! Like a siren song, the idea has lured people on. And always, in the end, those who have sought power for its own sake have found disillusionment and disappointment.

In the days of the Apostles' ministry on earth, a magician named Simon sought to buy spiritual power from Peter. The big fisherman rebuked him strongly, saying, "Your silver perish with you, because you thought you could obtain the gift of God with money!" (Acts 8:20)

Truly, power is a gift of God, freely given, but it is a gift to be used under God direction only. Wrong use of the God-given power potential will bring disappointing or even disastrous results. But power, rightly exercised under the direction of the Christ, the God Self of each individual, will accomplish good beyond our present ability to imagine.

Power, we must understand, is not an end in itself, not a goal to be sought. Rather, it is simply a means that enables us to attain the end result of bringing forth God ideas on earth. It is not to be used for selfish gain or satisfaction of the personal ego, but for the forward spiritual movement of the whole. It is to be exercised not for the purpose of controlling others, but for the purpose of taking dominion over our own thoughts and feelings in order to come into a greater God-awareness. It is a gift of God, and as such it must be respected and utilized to further His good work on earth.

With this in mind, then, let us see how we can go about developing our God-given potential of spiritual power under the direction of the Christ of our own being. Power is one of the twelve attributes of man to be awakened by our higher Self and developed as part of our spiritual nature. It is an important gift, but it is to be used in conjunction with the other eleven qualities in man.

Power is the vital energy that has its seat in the hollow of the throat, at the root of the tongue. Spiritual power flows into our body from the Christ center at the top of the head and is released in the form of radiant energy through the center in the throat. This quality is closely associated with the larynx, which contains the vocal cords, and the thyroid gland, which regulates growth. Power is released by consciously speaking positive, powerful words of Truth. A vibratory force is set free in mind and body by knowingly using such words as *God, power,* and *God-power.*

Try it for yourself. Walk back and forth, saying, "God!" Say it out loud. Over and over, with every step, say, "God!" Then feel the surge of vital energy in and through your whole being, released by the word of Truth. This is what Jesus meant when he said, "The words that I have spoken to you are spirit and life" (Jn. 6:63).

As a matter of fact, power is an activity or faculty that responds quickly to the command of the Christ, or the spiritual Self, in us. When we are in tune with God, we can quickly and easily release vital energy for any good purpose. We see the readiness of power to respond when we consider the story of how Jesus called Philip, the disciple who represents power.

It is told simply in the book of John: "The next day Jesus decided to go to Galilee. And he found Philip and said to him, 'Follow me'" (Jn. 1:43). Philip not only came himself, but even brought a friend, Nathanael. So the center of spiritual power is awakened by the Christ.

Later, after the resurrection and ascension of Jesus, Philip became noted for his ability to spread the message of Truth as a speaker. He traveled to various places, releasing spiritual power through the center of speech. His influence was great. On one occasion, in Samaria, it was reported that "the multitudes with one accord gave heed to what was said by Philip, when they heard him and saw the signs which he did" (Acts

8:6). So it is natural that he should be associated with the idea of power and its ganglionic center in the throat.

While all twelve powers are to be developed in harmony, some of them are more closely related than others. We discover the relationship by considering the disciples who represent them, as well as their centers in the body. Philip was a fisherman, as were several other disciples, and he and the brothers Andrew and Peter, who represent strength and faith, came from the same hometown, Bethsaida. Power is closely allied with faith and strength.

In order to reach the center in the throat through which power is loosed, the light from the I Am center at the top of the head passes through the ganglionic aggregate in the middle of the head, which is the seat of faith. Faith is absolutely necessary to the release of spiritual power. Without faith, little is accomplished.

Power and strength are also related and may be confused if not properly understood. Strength is endurance, stability, stamina. Power is the vital energy that enables us to accomplish, to follow through, to do.

Let us compare power and strength, qualities in man, to power and strength in electricity. Electrical energy flows over a wire to bring us an output of power. Strength is the quality of the conductor, or wire, over which the current flows. Power is the energy itself.

In our body, mind, and affairs, we must have strength as a basis for all activity. Without stability of purpose, strength of character, and physical endurance, we do not provide a clear and harmonious channel through which power can flow. Strength and power must be developed together.

By its location in the body, power is also closely linked with the faculty of zeal—power at the hollow of the throat and zeal at the base of the brain and the back of the neck. It is through increasing our zeal, or enthusiasm, for spiritual activity that we release more vital energy to accomplish the good we want to do. However, we must learn to temper our zeal with wisdom and use our power under God direction. If we become carried away with zeal and invest all our time and effort in trying to pass on spiritual power to others, we will find that we are neglecting ourselves. Charles Fillmore warns, "Do not put all your enthusiasm into teaching, preaching, healing, and helping others; help your own soul" (*RW*, p. 216).

The first outpouring of spiritual power may so awaken our desire to share the Truth that we are tempted to overextend ourselves in trying to pass it on to others. But we can only serve as channels for power. We cannot store it and then release it. We must keep both ends of the passage open if we are to have spiritual power available for our use.

As electrical energy is generated at the moment we turn the switch to call on it, so we serve simply as conductors of spiritual energy, or vital power. It is through opening the inlet by prayer and receptivity to God that we fill our power channel to release good into our world. Power cannot be stored. It can only be used. Since this is the case, we start to develop the power faculty, our ability to receive and use God energy, through learning to control our thoughts and feelings, opening ourselves to God-ideas in prayer, and seeking to come into harmony with God's way of life.

Jesus went apart to pray and came back refreshed and revitalized with greater spiritual power than ever. On the most important occasion of his life on earth, he took time to go into the garden of Gethsemane to pray, to prepare himself for that which was to come. Can we do less?

Fillmore explains: "To man is given the highest power in the universe, the conscious power of thought. There is a universal, creative force that urges man forward to the recognition of the creative power of his individual thought. . . . When he cooperates with Principle, man sits on the throne of his authority and the elemental force is subject to him" (*RW,* p. 151).

First within, and then without. This is the way we develop the power faculty. And we must continue to build from within, because this is the only way we can keep the inlet of this channel open. In order to use power, we must leave the way open for it to flow through. "Power is essential to the work that Jesus Christ expects his followers to do in the great field of humanity," but man is to exercise power first over "the multitudinous thought people of his own soul and body" (*TM,* p. 61).

These are the steps by which we develop our power channel:

I. Control

The development of power starts with control, and control begins with choice.

To control means "to exercise authority over; direct; command." The development of power must always start with control. Our purpose is to strengthen the channel and open the way for spiritual power to flow. We do this by exercising control—not over others or over our world, but over ourselves.

We direct or command our thoughts and feelings. Those which do not belong to us as a child of God are banished with a nonresistant thought of rejection, and those which help to convey to us the idea of our innate divinity are cultivated and encouraged. Daily, hourly, momently we make the choices that prepare us to be good stewards of spiritual power. Actually, it is the first awakening of the power faculty that enables us to establish control over our thoughts, words, and feelings.

By believing in our innate power, we refuse to say, "I can't help thinking—" or, "I can't help feeling—." Instead, we exercise the authority of our spiritual nature by determining for ourselves what we will think and what we will feel, and our awakening faculty provides the vital energy to back us up.

2. Poise

Through learning to control our thoughts and feelings, we develop poise. Poise is controlled power, energy that is waiting to be released for a chosen activity. This is still preparatory for the outpouring of unlimited spiritual power, but it is necessary as a part of awakening this quality.

For these first two steps, we must remember to keep a relaxed attitude toward the development of this vital energy idea. It is easy to become tense and try to force power. But power cannot be forced. It can only flow through the channel that is open to it. Relaxation opens the channel, and control helps to establish it.

Then, as we exercise authority over our thoughts and feelings, we become poised, balanced, stable, and we begin moving with ease and dignity. We do not fidget nor feel the need for constant movement and nervous mannerisms. There is a quiet control over mind and body that is not passive, but rather alert, waiting to be guided into greater fulfillment of God's good.

3. Accord

After we have taken command and established control in our lives we are ready to reach out for greater experiences in a spirit of agreement with the good everywhere. We will never be ready to receive spiritual power until we are in harmony with God; with the God potential, or good, in all persons; and with the basic principle on which our universe operates.

This again is a part of preparing ourselves for the responsibilities that come to us with the outpouring of vital energy through us. When we have established control and poise and are in accord with divine ideas, then we are ready for the further awakening of this spiritual activity.

4. Enduement

This is our first real experience of receiving spiritual power, feeling it flow through the God channel that we are becoming. Jesus prepared his disciples for this experience by telling them, "You shall receive power when the Holy Spirit has come upon you" (Acts 1:8).

After the Ascension, the disciples prepared themselves by meeting together for prayer, seeking to cleanse their thoughts and feelings, and consecrating themselves to do God's work. And on the holy day of Pentecost, as they prayed, they received a firsthand experience of spiritual activity. As long as Jesus was with them, they had looked to him as their power source. Now they learned to awaken the power center within their own being and "were all filled with the Holy Spirit and began to speak in other tongues, as the Spirit gave them utterance" (Acts 2:4).

So it will be for us. We may not have the experience that the Apostles described as a vision of fire and the sound of rushing wind. It may simply come as a feeling of new strength and life and joy, a greater ability to cope with life and increased energy to do the work God has given us. But this is the first awakening of spiritual power within us.

We must be sure to remember that this vital energy is not given to us to use for personal gain, but for the greater expression of God on earth. As we use the power we are receiving in a divinely ordered way, we increase our ability to call on it as needed.

5. Power

At this point we are receiving spiritual power in a continuing supply, and we are using it under God direction. It is only by right use that we continue to keep the channel open. As we master this step in development of the attribute, we are a good conductor, and the power flows through us in a continuous, unfailing stream.

We have opened the power channel, and we keep it open by taking time for rest, renewal, and revitalization of our whole being through regular prayer activity.

6. Dominion

After proving our discipleship and apostleship on the lower levels, we come to the place of dominion. With authority and distinction, we take command of every situation as Jesus did. We exercise a dominion, though, that is based first in self-government, always subject to the guidance and direction of Spirit within us.

Here we are able to declare, as Jesus did after the Resurrection (his ultimate earthly demonstration in self-mastery), "All power is given unto me in heaven and in earth" (Mt. 28:18 KJV).

7. Mastery

In exercising dominion, we think in terms of having power. Moving one step further, we are no longer separated from the power—we *are* power. Here we are so completely identified with the Source of power that we no longer think in terms of receiving or having this vital energy or even of using it in the right way. We simply are one with the faculty of power in such a way that it flows through us into right expression in our life without our conscious effort. We have attained the step of mastery, a mastery that is so complete there is not even any temptation to return to human thinking or feeling. We are one with power.

Instructions

To develop your power faculty, start with the first step of control. It is important that you take each step in a divinely ordered succession, because in order to open the power channel, you must first prove yourself and develop a stable base for the use of this spiritual energy. Otherwise, you may find yourself destroyed or depleted by too great a flow of energy through a channel that is not strong enough to handle it.

Power is another of the gifts of God. Misuse it or use it only for your personal glorification and gratification, and you will be hurt by it. But let it grow and let it flow through you as God's clear channel of expression, and you are unlimited!

Starting with the level of "control," use these positive, powerful affirmative thoughts to climb the ladder. Speak the words out loud, feeling the vibration of the words through the power center in your throat. With your inner vision, hold the picture of the radiant Christ light flowing from the top of your head through the faith center to be released as spiritual power from the larynx at the root of the tongue.

When you feel that you have mastered one step, move up to the next. Use these words aloud and silently to develop the ideas in consciousness.

> Control: *Under God's direction, I carefully choose my thoughts, words, and feelings.*
> Poise: *As a child of God, I am spiritually poised in mind and body.*

Accord: *I live in harmony with all good in God's universe.*

Enduement: *Through prayer and consecration, I prepare
myself to receive spiritual power.*

Power: *Spiritual energy now flows through my mind and
body.*

Dominion: *All power is given unto me in heaven and in
earth.*

Mastery: *I am one with all power in the universe now.*

You are here to be a channel for God's power. You are needed
to do God's work. Develop this activity of Spirit by first establishing self-mastery and control, and you will find that you are
unlimited, because God is unlimited.

8

See
It
Right

I n Unity there is a saying: "To set it right, see it right!"

This is a clue to the proper use of our God-given faculty of imagination. In order to change conditions in our mind, body, and affairs, we must first transform the pictures we are holding in mind. Our life and affairs will always flow into the mold we make for them through the use of our inner picturing power. If we don't like the conditions we are attracting, we can change them by building new images with the eye of the mind, our faculty of imagination.

We have what amounts to a continuously running moving-picture show being shown on a screen in our mind. Here we view our world, review past events, and project future experiences. If we project flickering images of first one thing and then another into our inner theater, we will express or attract a mixture of experiences, good and bad, in our life. However, by learning to make the right use of this important faculty and by making sure it is continuously guided and directed by the Christ, or

God Self, of our being, we can develop an imagination that will not only serve us well, but will also provide tremendous support in developing our other God-given powers.

Imagination makes its home in the body at a point between the eyes, where we might think of its function as that of a "third eye," one that enables us to see beyond what we normally take in through our two physical eyes. From the ganglionic center between the eyes, a line of communication runs back into the brain to connect with a picture-making function near the root of the optic nerve. As we seek to develop our power of imagination for God purposes, we concentrate our attention at this point between the eyes and encourage the awakening of our power to picture God-ideas.

The imagination serves us in several different ways. It supplements the work of the two physical eyes by interpreting, in the form of inner pictures, that which is seen. For instance, the face of a beloved person becomes beautiful to the soul of the one who loves, regardless of the human report of the physical eyes. Right use of the imagination in all areas of life and living will unearth beauty and goodness in the world not normally perceived by our human eyesight alone.

This inner eyesight also comes up with new pictures and possibilities by putting together known elements or experiences in new combinations. This is the way the imagination serves an inventor, for instance, in producing interesting possibilities for experimentation, all through the imaging power of the mind.

The imaging power also serves as a means of communicating ideas. How would we describe something or communicate an idea to someone else if that person had no ability to picture it? The one describing the item has a picture in mind that is conveyed to another by means of the image the second person makes on the screen of that person's mind. This is not a completely accurate means of communicating, because inner pictures are colored by the thoughts and feelings of the individual. But without this spiritual faculty, communication would be difficult indeed, if not impossible.

Imagination also serves the purpose (previously mentioned) of forming the design for the various facets of our lives. As within, so without—as in the picture chamber of our minds, so it will be in our world.

On the spiritual level, this important faculty is one means by which Spirit communicates with us, conveying to us the infinite powers and possibilities that are ours as children of God. Here we are able to release limiting thoughts and feelings by perceiving or glimpsing something greater, our divine potentiality. It may come to us first in the form of pictures. As we communicate with other people by describing mental images, so God communicates divine ideas and plans to us by projecting greater goals and good onto the screens of our minds.

Here, though, we must remember that the picture we receive from God is colored by our own mind conditioning. So it is to our advantage to purify our thoughts, feelings, and vision in order to be a clear channel through which the divine image comes in its original perfection. We do this by awakening, refining, and developing our God-given power of right inner vision.

In the symbology of the disciples as the twelve powers, awakened and evolved by Jesus as the Christ, Nathanael (Bartholomew) is the disciple who represents the imagination.

Nathanael, recruited by another disciple, Philip, was sitting under a fig tree, praying and meditating, as was customary in those days. Possibly, he was seeking greater understanding and a higher revelation of spiritual things.

At any rate, when Philip first approached him, Nathanael was skeptical about Jesus, and it wasn't until he actually met the man that he was convinced this was someone special, someone he could follow. Jesus casually mentioned that he had seen Nathanael under a fig tree before his friend called him. Perceiving that Jesus could have known this only through the power of inner vision (since he was out of sight of the Master), the newcomer exclaimed: "Rabbi, you are the Son of God! You are the King of Israel!" (Jn. 1:49)

Jesus then gave him the promise of the ultimate spiritual development of the imagination: "You shall see greater things than these. . . . Truly, truly, I say to you, you will see heaven opened, and the angels of God ascending and descending upon the Son of man" (Jn. 1:50-51).

Charles Fillmore explains Jesus' prediction in this way:

"With this spiritual faculty it is possible for man to penetrate into the 'fourth dimension' or what is usually called the 'kingdom of the heavens' and to discern the trend of the spiritual forces. The angels of God are spiritual forces active in the Sons of God, the spiritually quickened. The open and receptive and believing mind can see the things that take place in the Christ

Mind, thus transcending the capacity of the unillumined natural man" (*MJ,* p. 23).

Angels are frequently mentioned in the Bible as the means by which God communicates with us. Jacob, in his dream at Bethel, saw angels ascending and descending a ladder reaching to heaven. This was his first real revelation from God, in which he learned that God was everywhere. This Truth was imparted to him through the picturing power of the mind functioning in his dream.

God sometimes speaks to us in the pictures of our dreams. He also may convey a message through means of a vision. Dreams and visions are not to be sought as spiritual experiences, but may be used as guideposts along the way, correctly interpreted by understanding, which, you will remember, is another God faculty located in the head, not far from the seat of the imagination.

When the angels visit us in the form of the "imaging power of the mind receiving divine ideas and reflecting them into the consciousness" (*RW,* p. 13), we should welcome them as messengers of God and let them guide us into greater experiences of God's good. However, they are simply messengers. Spiritual visions are not to be sought as ends in themselves. And the power of the imagination is to be encouraged and developed always under the guidance of the Christ. The imagination is given to us to use; it should not make us its servant.

Imagination cannot be forced. It must be invited. Relaxation is important to keep the channels open in developing all the twelve powers, but it is especially necessary in working with the perceiving power within us. Thinking happy thoughts, expecting good, and opening yourself to God-ideas will set the stage for harmonious, prophetic images on the screen of your mind. And your God-given imaging power will serve you well.

The following are the steps through which we develop this faculty, starting with the step of cleansing old, false images, and culminating in the realization of spiritual vision, seeing as God sees.

I. Cleansing

Had we always employed our faculty of imagination correctly, picturing only God-ideas, we would not need this first step. But inasmuch as humankind as a whole has made wrong use of this imaging faculty in the past, we must learn to cleanse the screens of our minds so that we will not be confused by inharmonious, conflicting pictures.

Without thinking about it, just stop for a moment and close your eyes. What is playing on the screen of your mind today? Could it be the remembrance of some past injustice? Something feared? Some tragedy that might happen? If so, then this is the place you must start to train your imaging power correctly, by getting rid of the old, false ideas that will result in a double exposure when you try to superimpose thoughts of health and life and joy and peace and harmony.

Don't make a hard job of it. Under no circumstances should you fight or resist those negative pictures that may seem to be so real and powerful. With a simple thought of rejection, mentally erase them from your mind. Remember, *you are in charge.* In your Christ nature, you are developing and training these powers. Your imagination is here to serve you, and it will obey your orders if you are firm but nonresistant in dealing with the old, wrong images of the past.

Of course, the screen of your mind cannot remain a blank. So after erasing the limiting, error-filled images of the past, you must replace them with positive, powerful images that you want to see expressed in your life. In developing your faculty of imagination, you will want to work on the first two steps simultaneously.

And don't think that you can simply *forget* about cleansing as you advance further up the ladder. Buried in your subconscious mind are images from the past that may suddenly loom up to haunt you, even as you move ahead into new and greater experiences with your imaging power. When some picture that activates fear or a feeling of injustice or any negative feeling flashes on the screen of your mind, don't fight it. Just handle it with a simple, nonresistant thought of rejection, and continue on with the training and right use of your faculty of imagination.

2. Consideration

The more you become interested in showing yourself pictures of happy, healthy, prosperous, joyous experiences, the easier it becomes to forget the old, limiting pictures of the past.

However, don't hurry into the new concepts. Your imagination must be led. It cannot be forced. Consider what you want to express. With your eyes closed, project images on the screen of your mind. See yourself healthy, happy, and free. Does that seem difficult, all at once? Then break it down a bit. Give some thought to what it means to be healthy and happy. Picture yourself with a smile on your face. Consider the image you want to present to the world, and refine it with your inner eye. Look at it from all angles. Deliberate about it. Fill in the details. Literally build it into the image you want to express.

Interest in the new picture will help with the cleansing of old, unwanted images. Here you can "worry in reverse." Instead of picturing all the wrong things which might happen, draw inner images of all the good which is yours as a child of God.

3. Discrimination

Building new thought images will not remove you from the world, and from time to time you will find your inner eyesight picking up pictures presented to it by the world. Someone mentions a tragedy or even goes into detail about something that has happened, and your imagination, projecting the story from past experience, begins to play a film in your mind in keeping with the negation presented.

By mounting the step of discrimination, you learn to sort out immediately those ideas you want to accept and those you want to reject. Even though you have brought yourself carefully through the attitude of cleansing, you may still find that unbidden images arise, stimulated by something happening in your environment. Some of them even wear sheep's clothing. For instance, friends may insist so strongly that you become wrapped up in some negative situation that you feel almost guilty about not allowing it to show on the screen of your mind. But you are best able to help others when you maintain your own inner balance and right use of the picturing power. Remember, what you see is what will express itself. So see it right!

Discriminate. Learn to recognize differences and sort out the images you admit to your mind.

4. Observation

One of the ways to keep your imagination on the true and the good is to make it a point to observe, or watch for, the good everywhere—within and without.

Your imagination works from experiences and brings them forth in your life. These may be real or imaged, but the faculty produces them whether they are true or false. So the more you observe, pay attention to, and incorporate the good pictures in your thought and feeling, the more you will be expressing life, love, peace, and harmony. Train your physical eyesight to work from your inner eyesight and see the good, even in situations where there doesn't seem to *be* any good.

Observation is a matter of training yourself to fill your mind so full of right concepts that you literally crowd out any other pictures. Your awakening faculty of imagination helps you to do this. This is a step in mind training, preparatory to the spiritual awakening of the inner eyesight.

5. Beholding

From observation we move up to beholding—seeing our world in the light of Truth, or true ideas, the spiritual awakening of this attribute.

Charles Fillmore explains: "We are transformed by beholding. Whatever we persistently behold we manifest. Our looking into the perfect pattern, the indwelling Christ, and beholding His perfection transforms us into His likeness" (*RW,* p. 22).

All things are transformed as we see them with our spiritual eyesight, and we behold the true picture, regardless of what appears to be. At this point there still may be times when old, false images pop up from the subconscious, but we handle them easily in the light of Truth and continue to behold God in everything.

6. Discernment

Through our awakening spiritual faculty of imagination, we see past appearances to the Truth. But then we go one step further. We begin to perceive certain truths through a spiritual illumination above and beyond anything we have ever known: "Then shall your light break forth like the dawn" (Is. 58:8).

Here we may receive insight in the form of dreams or visions—or as direct revelation of Spirit. Fillmore defines spiritual discernment as "that inner spiritual faculty by which man may receive the revelations of God-Mind" (*RW,* p. 55). This is the highest function of the imagination, to enable us to receive God-ideas on the screens of our minds.

7. Vision

From the experience of having discernment, the ability to receive images from God, we advance to spiritual vision, the state of being so at one with the Source that we see with the eyes of Spirit. We no longer need to receive images as messages from God. Rather, we look with perfect sight, without thinking about it.

Fillmore describes spiritual vision as "seeing God as the foundation of all, the sources of all, and the substance of all. Seeing the good, the true, and the beautiful everywhere" (*RW*, p. 205). Here we have the "single eye," recommended by Jesus, without conscious thought or effort. We are one with God, and we see as He sees.

Instructions

Imagination must be invited, encouraged, and led. It cannot be forced. Remember this as you unfold the faculty first in a mental and then in a spiritual way.

Think of the seat of the imagination between the eyes as a third eye, with which you not only project inner images, but also correctly interpret the things you see with your physical eyes. Correct development of this power will orient you into a whole new world of experience, because seeing things right will set many things right in your world. To advance in the steps for the development of this faculty, use the following statements: Remember to work on cleansing and consideration together

and to return to the cleansing thought whenever necessary in
your progress.

>Cleansing: *I erase from the screen of my mind all false im-
>ages.*
>Consideration: *I reflect on pictures in keeping with my
>spiritual goals.*
>Discrimination: *Under God direction, I sort out the im-
>ages in my mind. I keep the good and discard the
>false.*
>Observation: *I observe good in action in my world.*
>Beholding: *I behold the Christ in myself and in all other
>persons and situations.*
>Discernment: *I accept spiritual insight from God.*
>Vision: *My eye is single to the good.*

In the preceding chapter we worked on the development
of the power channel. Now use the power that has been given
to you as a child of God to take control of your imaging faculty.
You will not only find yourself projecting good and interesting
pictures on the screen of your mind, but you will also be receiving spiritual revelations beyond anything you have dreamed
was possible.

And while the pictures change in your mind, your body and
circumstances are changing too. Because when you see it right,
you set it right!

Build Something to Stand On

When Jesus was twelve years old, his parents took him with them to Jerusalem. It was a happy, festive occasion—the Feast of the Passover—and when it was over, the group of relatives and friends from Galilee started home together.

At the end of the first day's journey, the boy's mother and father looked for him among the others and could not find him. So they went back to Jerusalem to search for Jesus. After three days they found him in the temple, "sitting among the teachers, listening to them and asking them questions" (Lk. 2:46).

Jesus was surprised at the concern of his parents over his disappearance. He was doing what came naturally to him—seeking a greater spiritual understanding. On this occasion of his first opportunity to visit Jerusalem, he sought out the most learned men of the time and listened to them and asked questions as they taught. "And all who heard him were amazed at his understanding and his answers" (Lk. 2:47). To him, even as a boy of twelve, it seemed the most natural thing in the world to take advantage of the opportunity to increase his knowledge and understanding of spiritual matters.

Understanding is important in developing our spiritual nature, because it is the faculty which puts feet under our prayers and gives our spiritual activity something to stand on. Blind faith, faith without understanding of the spiritual laws, may get results on occasion, but our spiritual growth demands a base that is more dependable. This can only be understanding that is grounded in spiritual Truth.

Jesus developed understanding and the other eleven powers or faculties within himself, and then he called the twelve disciples, who represent these ideas in mind.

Thomas Didymus is the disciple who stands for the faculty of understanding. A study of his contact with Jesus gives us some insight into the way we must develop our own ability to think and learn to make deductions and draw conclusions so that we may awaken this spiritual quality in us.

Thomas didn't always have spiritual understanding, but he wanted to learn. He didn't mind asking questions, and he listened to Jesus' answers. He needed to know. He wanted to know. As Jesus had questioned the learned men in Jerusalem, so Thomas questioned his teacher, Jesus Christ.

When the Master spoke of going away and of the other rooms in his Father's house, Thomas had to know more. He asked, "Lord, we do not know where you are going; how can we know the way?" (Jn. 14:5) His question showed that he was paying attention and thinking logically, and his interest was rewarded.

Jesus gave him the tremendous teaching, "I am the way, and the truth, and the life" (Jn. 14:6), pointing to the role of the inner Christ in revealing the spiritual way.

Thomas is probably best known for doubting the news of the Resurrection when he heard it secondhand from the other disciples. Jesus respected Thomas' need to know firsthand. Thomas was with the disciples when Jesus appeared to them on a later occasion. Jesus said to the doubter, "Put your finger here, and see my hands; and put out your hand, and place it in my side; do not be faithless, but believing" (Jn. 20:27). At last Thomas had advanced past the intellectual pursuit of knowledge, good in itself but always incomplete. And he exclaimed, with spiritual perception, "My Lord and my God!" (Jn. 20:28)

The awakening of our own faculty of understanding starts with questioning—questioning the old ways of thinking that may have been taken for granted, wondering about the "way" and the "truth," desiring to know—above all else, desiring to know the spiritual Truth. The desire for understanding leads to thinking about what is learned and seeking to put it all together in a body of information that will provide a basis for living.

Understanding is different from another of the faculties, wisdom, and it is well to note this difference. Charles Fillmore defines wisdom as "intuitive knowing; spiritual intuition" (*RW,* p. 211), and understanding as "the ability of the mind to apprehend and realize the laws of thought and the relation of ideas one to another"(*RW,* p. 202).

To put it more simply, wisdom knows, with the great white light of pure knowing. Understanding knows why. It sees the relationship between the parts of God's universe. It perceives the operation of spiritual laws. It puts everything together and comes up with the answers that stand under and support, first, the intellectual deduction, and finally, the spiritual conclusion.

The seat of spiritual understanding is in the front brain, very close to the I Am or Christ center at the top of the head. Understanding must be closely allied with the Christ, or it will be led astray by wrong reasoning and false conclusions.

It is also close in area to the will, which is located at a ganglionic center in the front forehead. Will and understanding are to be developed together, the understanding guiding the will and the will inspiring the understanding to action. Faith and imagination, whose centers also are in the head, must be called into play as a part of spiritual development of the faculty of understanding.

In awakening the understanding, it is good to remember that there is another center which represents this attribute: the part of the body that stands under the whole—the feet. The attention should be directed both to the feet and to the center at the front brain as we work to unfold this spiritual quality.

We must have the spiritual understanding which lifts us above the world, but also we must develop the base which enables us to relate to our world in a spiritual way. Thus, through developing a deep and sound base, we have something to stand on as we handle the situations that arise in our life experiences. The feet, according to Fillmore, "represent the phase of understanding that connects us with the outer or manifest world and reveals the right relationship toward worldly conditions in general" (*RW,* p. 74).

We must be careful, though, to leave our understanding free to expand. We are not to clothe our understanding of the right relationship to the world in shoes of limited thought. We must leave them free to be directed from the seat of spiritual understanding at the top of the head.

In developing this faculty, we must remember to employ our God-given ability to relax. Some people, trying hard to understand, become tense and anxious. Understanding does not come with force. It comes with a dedicated desire and interest, carried out in the intellectual learning activity. Then the prayerful awakening of the spiritual power comes about through our relaxed desire to know more, to relate in a better way to our God, ourselves, and our world. Thomas' desire to know was never quite fulfilled until he relaxed into the realization of spiritual illumination and recognized Jesus in his true spiritual identity.

Since the center of this faculty is located in the head, trying to force the awakening of the faculty will result in headaches. But also, since it is in the front brain, not far from the Christ center, letting God-ideas revolve and unfold in mind will result in a tremendous illumination of the whole being. The illumination that comes with increased insight also gives a feeling of lightness in the body, a release of darkness and heaviness. There will be a new understanding of yourself and your relationship to your world that may result in changes in your physical living habits, as well as in your mental and spiritual activities. Don't start the process of developing understanding unless you are willing to change, ready to "be renewed in the spirit of your minds, and put on the new nature, created after the likeness of God in true righteousness and holiness" (Eph. 4:23-24).

The steps in developing spiritual understanding are these:

1. Questioning

Thomas began his search for greater understanding by questioning—questioning of the old ways, questioning as a means of defining the new ideas being presented. He was a thinker, and he had to have a logical basis for what he believed.

So must we, if we would build the foundation for spiritual understanding. We cannot carry with us along the path of Truth the old concepts based on the way of the world, the acceptance of appearances, or even the well-meant insistence of others on a belief in limitation. We must be willing to question and then to break through the outdated ways of thinking in order to prepare a place for the new concepts and attitudes in mind.

Questioning, as the first step in developing understanding, does not reflect a belligerent attitude, but rather an interested desire to know. We think. We ponder. We wonder. We ask questions and seek new answers and insight.

We ask. Then we listen and consider and think about the answer when it comes. This is the way we learn and begin to compile our knowledge into a new picture—a new, harmonious whole.

Remember, too, that the greatest prerequisite to spiritual understanding is the sincere desire which motivates our search.

2. Perception

This step represents an intellectual grasp of spiritual concepts, which is gained through consistent, conscientious study. Because we want to know, we are not only inspired to learn, but we also must make a real mental effort to lay hold of the truths that are presented to us.

Again, we must remember not to try to force, not to become tense about our spiritual seeking. Rather, we are to read, study, learn, and take in the basic Truth ideas in the spirit of adventuring into a new world of knowledge and understanding.

This is still an intellectual approach to awakening the faculty, but it is a natural follow-up to the process of questioning and listening. The knowledge gained through perception will be basic to further development of this power.

3. Deduction

From the knowledge we have taken in, we begin to draw conclusions and to seek further answers by means of deduction. Through this process, we now ask ourselves questions, questions that enable us to come up with new answers, new insights, new conclusions. We may take a basic Truth idea and remove it from the realm of theory to the area of practical application as we form certain conclusions based on what we have learned and act on them.

The word *deduction* means "reasoning from the general to the specific, or from a premise to a logical conclusion." As a part of deduction, we will be working particularly with the step of meditation in prayer. Fillmore defines meditation as a "steady effort of the mind to know God" (*RW,* p. 131). As we meditate, we take the Truth ideas that we know and let them revolve in mind and unfold new meanings and insight to us. We encourage further deductions and new conclusions as we give time and attention to our search for greater insight and deeper understanding. This step on the intellectual level leads us to an awakening beyond that which is known or learned from books and teachers.

4. Prophecy

Prophecy is an awakening of the faculty that is referred to by Fillmore as "quickening of the intellect . . . or intellectual illumination that precedes the awakening of the ideal, the Christ understanding." He explains this ability to prophesy as follows:

"There is in man a knowing capacity transcending intellectual knowledge. Nearly everyone has at some time touched this hidden wisdom and has been more or less astonished at its revelations. It certainly is a most startling experience to find ourself giving forth logical thoughts and words without preparation or forethought, because we nearly always arrive at our conclusions through a process of reasoning. However, the reasoning process is often so swift that we are likely to think that it is true inspiration" (*TM,* p. 88).

John the Baptist had this ability to prophesy. As a matter of fact, it was believed by many that John was the reincarnation of Elijah, one of the prophets of the Old Testament.

This awakening of our understanding, which enables us suddenly to see the answer without consciously thinking it through, may please us so much that we are tempted to stop right here, not seeking to develop our powers further.

Here also there may be the temptation to use our insight and our ability to prophesy to condemn others, to delight in our understanding of the law that enables us to know that others will be punished by their own mistakes and wrong actions. John brought about his own death as the result of using his power of prophecy in this way. He condemned Herod Antipas, the king of Galilee, for his illegal marriage to his brother's wife, Herodias, and thus inspired the intense hatred that resulted in his death.

This prophet who foretold Jesus' coming accomplished much good, but he was limited, because his understanding was still on the intellectual plane. Though illumined, the faculty was limited.

Even John recognized this. Speaking of Jesus, he said, "He must increase, but I must decrease" (Jn. 3:30). We must not be content to stay at the level of prophecy. We cannot afford to take this intellectual illumination as final but must continue to seek the inner light of spiritual comprehension and with it the love that erases all tendencies to judge or condemn. This leads us to the first true spiritual level of development.

5. Compassion

Understanding is perfected in love, and without love, it cannot be completely awakened in a spiritual way. On the level of compassion, understanding is tempered and given new depth by the activity of love.

Fillmore explains it this way: "Man receives first an intellectual understanding of Truth which he transmits to his heart, where love is awakened. The Lord reveals to him that the faculty of love is the greatest of all the powers of man and that head knowledge must decrease as heart understanding increases" (*TM*, p. 91).

Understanding, as well as wisdom, must work with love, or it will be cold and unfeeling. But an understanding heart provides the insight that enables one to continually produce the right answers, as Solomon did.

Compassion is not sympathy, which includes an identification with the wrong, but rather a forgiving, understanding love that sees past the error to the Truth, without any feeling of condemnation for the expression of limitation.

6. Understanding

Compassion awakens further potentialities of mind that result in the next advancement, to spiritual understanding, which Fillmore defines as "the quickening of the Spirit within" and "the ability of the mind to apprehend and realize the laws of thought and the relation of ideas one to another" (*RW*, p. 202).

This ability enables us to see clearly in all matters, to receive instant answers to our questions, and to provide the proper and orderly planning and motivation for action by the will. It provides something to stand on and is translated into right decisions that result in right relationships and conditions in our daily activity and our world.

7. Illumination

The highest development of the faculty of understanding is illumination, a state of oneness in which we live in the light of clear and perfectly developed spiritual understanding. No longer do we ask questions; it isn't necessary. The answers are there, and before we ask, we know. The inner light of Truth shines clearly, setting us free from the need to ask. Here the illumined consciousness, "a mind purified by the light of Truth," is continually filled with illumined thought, "thoughts quickened through their conscious relationship to Spirit" (*RW*, p. 103).

Instructions

Awakening the faculty of understanding in a spiritual way is an activity that will change not only your way of thinking, but also your way of life. Be prepared for this as you question, study, and even pass the level of prophecy to go on to greater discoveries of Truth. There is a Spirit in you that has all the answers. Trust it as you proceed in an orderly, harmonious, loving way to unfold this faculty.

These are the statements for advancement up each step:

Questioning: *I am willing to question old beliefs for the purpose of satisfying my desire for spiritual understanding.*

Perception: *I consciously take hold of spiritual concepts.*

Deduction: *I meditate on the spiritual Truth I know.*

Prophecy: *My mind is quickened by new revelations of Spirit.*

Compassion: *The truth that I know is now rooted and grounded in love.*

Understanding: *I see, feel, and understand all things in the light of Spirit.*

Illumination: *The light of perfect understanding illumines my life.*

The light of understanding may come slowly, or it may come quickly as you follow through on your search. But it is well worth the price of concentrated attention and dedicated development.

From time to time, as you hold the thought for taking your next step up, take your attention away from the nerve center in the front brain and let it drop to your feet. Say, *My feet are placed on the firm rock of understanding.* When your understanding is developed in both head and feet, not only will you have the light in mind, but you will also have the ability to apply it in your world.

Understanding is another of the gifts of God, and it is one that is basic in development of all the other faculties.

10

Re-Educate
Your Executive
Faculty

"I n the present state of race consciousness, all people use the intellectual will to excess" (*TM,* p. 108). So Charles Fillmore points to the prevalent preoccupation of the human executive faculty with selfish aims and goals. It is our job in developing our God-given potentialities to re-educate the will, the directing power of our mind, to teach it to become receptive to spiritual motivation, rather than to goals determined by our materialistic pursuits alone.

The world makes its claims. If we are not careful, we may let those claims determine our decisions, even choose our aims in life, instead of developing our inner ability to exercise dominion over ourselves and our world. One way or another, we are using our will, our executive mind power, all the time. We choose a course of action. We resist or resent. We submit or fight back. We aim high or we slide backward. Or we are willing to consecrate and dedicate our will to God and to let it be re-educated to go His way.

Jesus was our great Way-Shower in overcoming the human, selfish motivation of the will and allowing it to be replaced by a great unification with the divine will, thus producing good for all. His greatest example in the area of re-educating the will was the prayer in the garden of Gethsemane, in which he said, "Not my will, but thine, be done" (Lk. 22:42).

This was not a prayer of submission to negation and suffering, as many people believe. Rather, it was a prayer of surrender to the all-wise, all-knowing Mind of God, in the realization that the fulfillment of the divine plan would bring good to all. From this point on, the crucifixion was not the important event in Jesus' mind. Rather, he was ready for the Resurrection, a complete overcoming of all human limitation. He was in a high state of consciousness that was in tune with the will of God so completely that his spiritual success was assured.

The rewards of unifying our wills with the will of God are great. They include health, happiness, joy, peace, harmony, prosperity, and other good that we cannot even visualize in our present state of consciousness. But the spiritual development of this executive faculty is something that requires much time, thought, and consecration. Had we always been close to God in our thinking, we would not have the long road to travel. But, as Charles Fillmore pointed out, the human race as a whole has developed the habit of letting its decisions and motivation be dictated by selfish human concerns. So we must break free of the race consciousness in order to build our ability to be in tune with God's will of good.

The first step is to correct our old thinking in regard to the will of God. Most people today are indoctrinated in a teaching that presents God as a stern, unyielding judge who arbitrarily brings difficulties, such as sickness and death, to His children.

God is not a person, and we are not to picture the Divine in our image and likeness. Rather, we should mold ourselves according to the spiritual nature God has placed within our own souls. When we begin to re-educate our thinking and learn to know our loving heavenly Father, we know that His will for us, His children, must be good. How could it be otherwise?

Jesus was seeking to help us understand this when he explained: "What man of you, if his son asks him for bread, will give him a stone? Or if he asks for a fish, will give him a serpent? If you then, who are evil, know how to give good gifts to your children, how much more will your Father who is in heaven give good things to those who ask him!" (Mt. 7:9-11)

No matter how we try, we will not be able to say with Jesus "Not my will, but thine, be done" until *we are able to believe that God's will for us is good.* We may speak the words, but we can only realize the prayer when we are joyously, enthusiastically in favor of having God's good plan made manifest in our lives.

God's will for us is good! We cannot overemphasize the importance of believing this wholeheartedly as the first step in re-educating our directing power of mind. As we begin to incorporate this concept in our conscious thinking, we must pass it along to the subconscious mind and re-educate all the old thought centers with the good news that God, our loving heavenly Father, desires only good for us.

By awakening our will and understanding centers in the front of the head to this Truth, we begin to transform our whole being.

The ganglionic focal point where the will is developed is in the middle of the forehead, very close to the seat of understanding in the front brain. These two powers are closely related and are to be awakened and trained together, always under the guidance of the Christ. Make sure these two nerve centers are wide awake and listening as you pass along the good news: "God's will for me is good, more good than I can begin to imagine in my human thinking." Then look around to see how this Truth applies in your life, your aims, and your relationships with others.

If God's will for you is good, then God's will for all of humanity is good. Realizing this Truth brings about changes in your attitude toward others.

Many inharmonies in human relationships result from the clash of human wills. Learning to activate the divine will in your life does not mean that you will simply submit to the human will of others. Instead, it will give you a new freedom that recognizes the human force applied by others but does not submit to it. Neither do you have to fight. You simply go ahead with resolution and do the work that needs to be done at the time.

When you find yourself confronted by a strong will that insists you go its way, turn within to the Christ, the God Self, the spiritual core of your nature, and silently say to the other person, "The Christ in me beholds the Christ in you." Let the love of God and the understanding of the spiritual nature of that other person pour forth from you so strongly that there is no conflict of human wills. Rather, there is a higher power at work, establishing harmony and order.

Of course, while you do not allow another to direct your life, you must also be willing to give *others* freedom. In the case of children, you give them loving direction. When you are obedient to Spirit, you will find it is not necessary to have violent confrontations of will in order to train a child in the right way.

In your relationships with adults, you will have a new sense of freedom. While you will use wisdom and understanding in dealing with others, you will recognize that each must find individual fulfillment. This does not give anyone the right to take advantage of you or force his or her way on you. It does give each of us the privilege of choosing the religion which is right for us at this time, taking the job which we prefer, and in other ways making our own decisions and choosing the route we will take. As Fillmore reminds us, "We should remember that the right to exercise freedom of will was given to man in the beginning, according to Genesis, and that will should always be given its original power and liberty" (*TM,* p. 105).

It is interesting that the disciple who represents the faculty of will was a man who needed a strong human determination to do the job he did before joining Jesus. Matthew was a tax collector, one of the hated representatives of the Roman government, who collected taxes from the Jewish people. In order to continue in this particular line of work, Matthew had to be thick-skinned and determined.

But we find that even the will which has been wrongly directed in the past can be transformed immediately when touched by the Christ, represented by Jesus. When Jesus said to Matthew, "Follow me," the tax collector immediately "left everything, and rose and followed him" (Lk. 5:28).

The Hebrew meaning of the name *Matthew* is "given wholly unto Jehovah," and it is not until our will is completely dedicated to and directed by God that it serves us in the right way and enables us to fulfill our divine potential.

However, we can start first to awaken the will and train it by consciously watching its activities and directing it through our growing spiritual understanding. We are not to sublimate the will. We need it, working for us, but always in connection with the other closely related powers, all under the direction of the Christ.

Remember especially that the will and understanding, both working from centers in the front brain, must cooperate. Understanding on its own may do nothing. Will, on the other hand, may go ahead forcefully and do the wrong thing. Working in harmony together, the two faculties accomplish much. Will determines the movement; understanding decrees the direction.

These are the steps in developing the faculty of will to provide impetus for forward movement in the right direction. We start with simple methods of mind training and advance across the bridge to spiritual enlightenment.

1. Willingness

Willfulness, the human determination of the will to have its own way, must be replaced by willingness—the willingness to learn, to change, to cease resistance, to go God's way. Anyone who has been accustomed to forcing his or her way with human determination must consciously take this step as a giving up or releasing of old habits and attitudes.

This step is also important for persons who have been accustomed to letting others determine their way in life. Such individuals must consciously clear away the debris of old attitudes of inferiority and habits of taking the line of least resistance. For the first time, they may take a stand, do their own thinking, make their own choices, actually choose a whole new lifestyle. This is all for the good, and this, too, is a form of willingness, the first step in developing the executive faculty under God direction. This type of person will need to spend particular thought and effort on the next step (resolution) as well.

Whether we have in the past exercised a strong personal will or allowed ourselves to be dominated by others, we must be willing to learn God's way now.

2. Resolution

The word *resolution* has two meanings that are applicable here: "decision as to future action" and "a resolute quality of mind."

Will is our executive power of mind. It must be trained to take control and make decisions and then to stick with them and follow through on them. Here we determine the direction we will take and then establish the strength of determination to follow through on it, not in the human thought of getting our own personal way, but in the higher area of determining a path of spiritual growth. It is a decision that only we can make for ourselves.

3. Training

The will must be trained to do the work of bringing forth the new person. In order to be qualified to direct the activities of the other powers, it must be re-educated into right thinking, taught to make right decisions, and schooled to work under the direction of the growing spiritual understanding.

As the will is trained, it trains the other faculties, awakening them to the divine potential, watching the thoughts and feelings, and generally supervising the building of the new person. This is a continuing activity. Even as you advance further in the unfoldment of the faculty of will, you will need to continue to train and guide this faculty and, through it, the other faculties.

4. Obedience

Advancing beyond the intellectual training of our executive power, we approach the bridge to spiritual awakening. We must learn to be responsive to the voice of Spirit within. Charles Fillmore describes obedience as the "erasing of the personal man" (*TT,* p. 93) and "a letting go of pride, ignorance, selfishness, ambition, and the thousand and one dense ideas that make the soul opaque to the eye of Spirit" (*TT,* p. 93-94).

But suppose you reach this point and you aren't sure of the guidance of Spirit. Then simply continue to awaken your faculties through prayer and follow the best you know. As you continue to be true to your highest present understanding, you will awaken a greater awareness and comprehension. You will find that the will is instrumental in helping you to follow through on the highest and best you can see at this time, and your own sincerity, dedication, and obedience will open the way to realms of spiritual understanding.

5. Government

Having cleansed ourselves of willfulness, adopted a course of action toward spiritual aims and goals, and learned obedience to the best we know, we are now ready to exercise our faculty of will as the executive power it is.

We are no longer dependent on the opinions of others to make our decisions. We no longer resist or resent or try to force our human will on others. Neither do we let them choose our way.

The Old Testament prophet Isaiah spoke of the coming of the Messiah, and he proclaimed, "The government will be upon his shoulder, and his name will be called 'Wonderful Counselor, Mighty God, Everlasting Father, Prince of Peace.' Of the increase of his government and of peace there will be no end" (Is. 9:6-7).

Our will now functions under our own Messiah, the Christ, the spiritual nature, and His government increases as our executive faculty carries out orders from the headquarters of Spirit within us.

In the human consciousness, through the exercise of our human will, we can (and do) fail, no matter how forceful we are. In the divine consciousness, under God direction we are invincible. Even when we seem to fail in some human endeavor, we find that in the long run we have triumphed, as Jesus did.

At the time it seemed that the Crucifixion represented Jesus' failure, a giving in to the forces of the world. But the Crucifixion led to the Resurrection, which in the long run, turned out to be the greatest triumph of all time, more far-reaching than any other single event in human history.

When the government is upon the shoulders of the Christ in us, then our will truly functions in a spiritual way; but we must take one step more to pass beyond all human involvement.

6. Surrender

Here we are able finally to give up all personal direction of the will as we say with Jesus, "Not my will, but thine, be done." This is not simply a matter of speaking words, but of being so completely in agreement with God's ideas that we are willing to trust Him and let Him direct our life in all departments, through the executive power of our minds.

This is not a negative sort of submission, but a positive activity in which we give all power to the Christ within us. We consciously choose to do this.

The rewards of surrender are great. Jesus told his followers: "Truly, I say to you, in the new world, when the Son of man shall sit on his glorious throne, you who have followed me will also sit on twelve thrones, judging the twelve tribes of Israel. And every one who has left houses or brothers or sisters or father or mother or children or lands, for my name's sake, will receive a hundredfold, and inherit eternal life" (Mt. 19:28-29).

When the twelve faculties are completely developed under the spiritual guidance of the Christ, the rewards will be beyond anything we can imagine. And directing this activity, we must have the will, taking its orders from Spirit within, completely in tune with the divine will.

7. Unity

Finally, we move past surrender into the ultimate oneness with the will of God. We no longer have to think about it or be conscious of it. We simply let our lives move in harmony with it.

Jesus did this. Fillmore explains: "It is possible . . . for man so to identify his consciousness with Divine Mind that he is moved in every thought and act by that Mind. Jesus attained this unity" (*TM,* p. 105). And so must we ultimately attain this point of unity.

Instructions

Developing the faculty of will in a spiritual way must be done in a relaxed, willing, expectant frame of mind. If you find that there is a tendency to become tense and to try to force this faculty, stop and take stock.

Tension and force are characteristics of the human will. It is our aim to unfold God's will in and through us. Relax. Be receptive to spiritual ideas. Be willing to go God's way. This is the way to "unity."

Use the following statements to help you advance each step in the spiritualization of your executive power of mind:

> Willingness: *I am willing to learn God's way.*
> Resolution: *I will to will the will of God.*

Training: *I invest my resources of mind and body in a program of spiritual training.*

Obedience: *In the light of God, I faithfully follow the best I know.*

Government: *God works in me to will and to do that which He would have me do—and God cannot fail.*

Surrender: *"Not my will, but thine, be done"—in all things.*

Unity: *I Am the will of God in expression.*

The center of the will is in the forehead, close to the understanding realm and not far from the seat of the Christ at the top of the head. Keep your attention on this area as you re-educate the executive power of your mind to unfold your divine potential in all areas of life and living.

Establish a Center for Order

Jesus told us about the birds, the flowers, and the grass of the field. He said: "Look at the birds of the air: they neither sow nor reap nor gather into barns, and yet your heavenly Father feeds them. . . . Consider the lilies of the field, how they grow; they neither toil nor spin; yet I tell you, even Solomon in all his glory was not arrayed like one of these. But if God so clothes the grass of the field, which today is alive and tomorrow is thrown into the oven, will he not much more clothe you, O men of little faith? Therefore do not be anxious, saying, 'What shall we eat?' or 'What shall we drink?' or 'What shall we wear?' . . . Your heavenly Father knows that you need them all. But seek first his kingdom and his righteousness, and all these things shall be yours as well" (Mt. 6:26, 28-33).

What is the secret of this order that we find in nature? Why is it that humankind, the highest form of life, seems to have so much difficulty in establishing harmony, right relationships, and orderly growth, while the animals, plants, and birds go right along living as they are intended to live, doing what they are supposed to do?

All lower life-forms have a built-in intelligence that enables them to adjust to their environment, complete a cycle of growth, and produce the results which are expected of them by virtue of their nature. Yet humans seem to run into problems in adjusting to their environment, getting along with others of their species, and fulfilling a worthwhile pattern in living. Why? How are humans different from the birds, trees, animals, and plants?

The answer is that we have been given freedom of choice, which Jesus seems to indicate in directing us to "seek first his kingdom." Humans have the choice to seek or not seek the kingdom. That choice is part of the divine order. Humans alone, as co-creators with God, can think consciously, make decisions (right or wrong), and determine the direction their lives will take. All other forms of life simply follow instinct. Only *we* can think for ourselves and say "I will" or "I won't."

We are charged to use this ability to think, reason, and choose wisely to establish an orderly growth for ourselves as God's highest creations.

The lower forms of life fulfill their purposes in living by cooperating with divine law. Instinctively, they know what to do, and they do it. Because we human beings have lived for so long in the world and allowed our thoughts and feelings to be dictated by the situations, things, and people around us, we must consciously return in mind to that place where we can experience harmony and balance, divine adjustment, and right relationships. We do this by awakening and training our center for order.

Order is one of our twelve powers, an essential part of our God-given potential. To develop divine order in our lives, we must learn to cooperate with spiritual law. Obedient cooperation with God's plan of good is the secret that clothes the lily with beautiful attire; and it is the secret that will make our lives happy, harmonious, and balanced.

"The earth produces of itself, first the blade, then the ear, then the full grain in the ear" (Mk. 4:28). So Jesus pointed to the orderly growth that is the method through which we develop our God-given potential. We start our study of Truth in an intellectual way. This is the "blade," the beginning of inner growth. Then, as spiritual ideas develop in mind, we come to the point represented by the "ear," the ripening fruit of prayer and spiritual seeking. Finally, we reach the fulfillment stage of "the full grain," the expression of Spirit through our whole nature, the point of oneness developed in each of the faculties.

We don't jump from "blade" to fullness of spiritual power overnight. We grow there. Orderly and harmonious cooperation with divine law leads to the orderly, harmonious unfoldment of our spiritual natures in the same sequence that nature follows in its growth.

Many people, when they first start the study of their twelve spiritual faculties, would like to see instant results. They want unlimited spiritual power to flow through their whole being. But our spiritual growth, as with all growth, is rooted in order.

Children are not ready for the responsibilities of an adult. We would not expect to leave them in charge of complicated machinery or make them lift heavy items. They simply aren't ready for these activities.

As children in spiritual growth, we must prepare to handle the complicated machinery of living by learning and growing in a small way. We can only lift the heavy items after we have practiced on lighter loads. Were we suddenly given an unlimited flow of spiritual power, not only would we not know how to handle it, we actually could be seriously hurt or even destroyed by it. Order is the key to growth. We start where we are, first learning intellectually about such God-given qualities as life and love and wisdom. Then we put them to work. We awaken their centers in our bodies, as we awaken the ideas in mind—until one day the centers are touched with spiritual light, and we know, we feel, we actually experience the work of the power in a spiritual way.

Order starts with the establishment of this concept in our thinking and then works from within out. Orderly thinking leads to right relationships, harmonious results, and divinely directed actions. Some people, in establishing order, think first in terms of urging their systems and methods on other people. This is not the purpose of this faculty. We must first work on ourselves and then, from harmonious, happy feelings within, bring forth God-ideas into our immediate environment. Under no circumstances are we to attempt to force outer order. Anytime that we find we are becoming tense, anxious, and forceful in developing any of our powers, we should immediately relax, get in tune with the divine idea, and put Christ in charge. Our first work is always done on ourselves.

In the case of order, once we have put ourselves in tune with God-ideas and are cooperating with divine Principle, we will find that we attract right relationships with other people, satisfying and fulfilling activity, time for all the things we need to do, and right growth and development of all our powers. Unfoldment of this divine attribute also enables us to find our right place in the orderly, overall scheme of things and to fulfill God's greatest plan for our lives.

The disciple who represents the faculty of order is James, the son of Alphaeus, sometimes called "James the Lesser." We don't know whether this disciple was called "the Lesser" because of his stature or because he was considered less prominent among the group than the other James, the son of Zebedee and brother of John. This James stands for the quality of wisdom. Since both disciples were called James, we see that the qualities they represent must be closely related.

Certainly, wisdom does seem to have more prominence than order among the twelve powers of man. As Peter, James, and John were with Jesus on many important occasions, so the faculties they represent (faith, wisdom, and love) may seem closest to the Christ in our spiritual development. However, as James the Lesser worked quietly among the disciples, so the faculty of order works with the other eleven powers to establish harmony, balance, and right relationships. Its function is one of cooperation with the other attributes in a process of orderly growth—not a spectacular activity, but an important one, nevertheless.

The ganglionic centers for the two Jameses are in proximity, and here, too, we see the need for close cooperation between the two faculties, wisdom and order. The son of Zebedee—wisdom, or judgment—resides in the pit of the stomach, while the son of Alphaeus, "the Lesser," works through the digestive organs and makes his home at a point just behind the navel.

Both judgment and order, wrongly directed, may lead to criticism, contention, force, and condemnation, if allowed to relate only to the human side of thinking and living. Judgment may condemn. Order may insist on having everything its own way. When the two powers are totally under the direction of the Christ, harmony and right growth and unfoldment will be established.

On the other hand, with wisdom and judgment (spiritually developed) providing the guidance and divine order supplying the pattern, we make forward progress at an unprecedented rate.

Anytime there is any problem with the digestive organs, it is well to check the application of these two powers. Condemnation, criticism, hurry, and worry—resulting in hit-and-run meals, antagonism, and other wrong interpretations of the God powers—will cause difficulties in the stomach and the digestive tract. Spiritual development of wisdom, cooperating with its brother—love—and working through order as well, will resolve such physical inharmonies. The three qualities—wisdom, love, and order—meet in the great central nerve center, the solar plexus region.

In training the faculty of order, we center our attention on the point just behind the navel and hold positive thoughts for right adjustment—first, in our thinking; next, in our feelings; then, in our activity; and, finally, in our spiritual unfoldment. Then we mentally link order with love and wisdom, with our attention on the solar plexus. The steps in developing our faculty of spiritual order and divinely unfolded growth are these:

1. Orientation

Orientation means "recognition of and adaptation to a situation or environment." This first step brings us to a point of ending all resistance to the world as it is and conditions as they are and begins our orientation into the spiritual world that lies behind all appearances. Through learning God's laws, we completely change our outlook. We do not try to force outer changes, but we begin to make inner changes in our thinking. We adjust our view of the world to a growing understanding of spiritual principle. And we make this process of adjustment one of orderly growth. We are preparing ourselves to cooperate with the divine pattern for our lives, just as the flowers, birds, and grass of the field do. And we are doing it through establishing new patterns of thought, new attitudes, and a whole new outlook on life.

At this point we must stop blaming other people or outer conditions for our problems and begin to orient ourselves to thinking in terms of divine law and orderly cooperation with it. This is, first, the conscientious transformation of our minds and revamping of our everyday thinking.

2. Consent

After orienting our thinking to harmonize with ideas of divine order, we must train our feeling nature as well. We do this by consenting to feel with the idea of a spiritual universe, taking personal responsibility, and cooperating with divine law as a way to spiritual mastery.

It is not enough to recognize these ideas intellectually. We must back up our mental acceptance with a feeling of agreement. The word *consent* is derived from Latin words meaning "to feel with." Our mental orientation to ideas of a spiritual world based on spiritual law must be backed up by our emotional acceptance of the whole idea. We must be willing to "feel with" this new concept.

3. Cooperation

From mental acceptance and emotional agreement, we progress to the activity phase of the development of our faculty of order.

Here we must establish, first of all, that we are not simply seeking to impose our methods and practices on others arbitrarily. Rather, we are to learn how to apply the principles we now have accepted mentally and agreed with in our feeling nature. We are to put them to work as a part of our daily experiences. It is a process of cooperating, or working with, the spiritual laws as we understand them. Again, it is well to remember what positive results the lower forms of nature attain by simply cooperating with the divine plan for their growth and unfoldment.

This is what Jesus meant when he said, "If you know these things, blessed are you if you do them" (Jn. 13:17). It is good to know. It is good to feel strongly about the Truth known. But it is the doing, the follow-through, that establishes order on a firm basis and brings us up to the bridge of spiritual awakening.

4. Harmony

Charles Fillmore explains, "The divine idea of order is the idea of adjustment, and as this is established in man's thought, his mind and affairs will be at one with the universal harmony" (*RW,* p. 143).

Harmony cannot be established in mind, body, or affairs except through our cooperation with divine Principle. All three of the earlier steps must be taken before we can begin to feel this sense of accord with God's good everywhere. We must think in terms of God's universe, founded on universal, spiritual law. We have to put ourselves in tune with it emotionally. Then we are to apply the Truth we know in our activity. And, finally, we reach this bridge to the spiritual awakening, where we actually feel a sense of harmony that establishes for us a new relationship with God's good everywhere.

Order must be based on harmony, or it is not order at all.

5. Order

Order is "a condition in which everything is in its right place and functioning properly." We can only experience this on the spiritual level.

Order established simply in a human way or imposed on others through force is not the true expression of this spiritual power, and it will attract confusion rather than orderly progression. But order based on enlightened cooperation with divine law and divine guidance brings about right adjustment and harmonious growth.

When we are at this level in the development of order, we are not standing still. Rather, we are progressing under God direction in a divinely unfolding way, continually bringing forth more and more of our divine potential in a balanced, harmonious manner.

6. Freedom

"You will know the truth, and the truth will make you free. . . . If the Son makes you free, you will be free indeed" (Jn. 8:32, 36).

In giving us this promise, Jesus pointed out the importance of establishing an orderly cooperation with divine Principle. He explained, "Every one who commits sin is a slave to sin" (Jn. 8:34). Sin is simply a mistake, a breaking of the laws of God's universe. Such error carries its own imprisonment.

The only true freedom is the freedom that comes to us through our spiritual awakening, as we put the Christ, the Son of God within us, in charge and work with Spirit in a divinely ordered way. Thus, the Son—working in and through our minds, bodies, and affairs—frees us to experience the fulfillment of life and growth.

Charles Fillmore says: "We can never know the full meaning of freedom until we abide in the Christ consciousness. . . . Liberation from bondage comes as we seek first the perfect Mind of Christ." He further explains that freedom is "a result of regulating one's life according to Principle, not according to what anyone else may think or say" (*RW,* p. 79).

7. Continuity

From the freedom that is the result of continuous, conscious, orderly cooperation with Christ ideas and spiritual guidance, we move to the step of oneness in the faculty of order. This is continuity.

Here we proceed in a sequence of expression of God in such a way that there is no sense of stopping to make decisions or consciously cooperating with divine law. Rather, there is such a realization of oneness with God's order that we unconsciously make right decisions and move forward in a continuous realization of harmony.

Fillmore explains it this way: "Divine Mind rests in a perpetual Sabbath, and that which seems work is not work at all. When man becomes so at-one with the Father-Mind as to feel it consciously, he also recognizes this eternal peace, in which all things are accomplished" (*TM,* p. 113) .

Instructions

Order is the outgrowth of our complete agreement and cooperation with spiritual law. This is a process that must be complete—in mind, in emotions, and in actions.

Unless you feel that you have already adjusted mentally to living in the spiritual, God-created universe, rather than in the world, you will want to start with the first step. Here you will adjust your thinking to the idea of living in the invisible, perfect world of Spirit, where you are learning to think in harmony with God's laws. Then you will progress through the levels of adjusting your feeling nature to this concept—learning to apply spiritual laws in your life. You will finally move across the bridge to spiritual realization of the quality of order.

Use the following statements to help you work out these steps in mind:

> Orientation: *I orient my thinking to a God-created universe, governed by spiritual law.*
> Consent: *I consent to do things God's way.*
> Cooperation: *Actively and enthusiastically, I cooperate with the laws of God's universe.*
> Harmony: *My thinking, my feeling, and my actions are all in harmony with God's laws, and I attract harmonious results.*
> Order: *I advance daily in a divinely ordered way.*
> Freedom: *I experience the freedom of the Christ consciousness.*
> Continuity: *I am one with the harmonious, continuous forward movement of God's universe.*

The goal of resting in the eternal Sabbath, in which all things proceed in a consciousness of peace and harmony, is well worth the dedication that is necessary to develop your order faculty.

12

Go

Forward

"Zeal is the impulse to go forward, the urge behind all things. Without zeal, stagnation, inertia, death would prevail throughout the universe. The man without zeal is like an engine without steam or an electric motor without a current" (*TM,* p. 130). So Charles Fillmore points to the importance of our God-given ability to be zealous, enthusiastic about life and living. He also details the limitation of a life that is lacking in the development of this faculty, comparing the person to "an engine without steam or an electric motor without a current."

Actually, as with all the twelve attributes of man, zeal has been given to each of us in bountiful measure. It is simply the failure of the individual to accept this free-flowing abundance that results in a life which is stagnant, limited, "without steam," pointless, dull, and disappointing.

The people of Laodicea were described in the book of Revelation as lacking in zeal. The angel was told to write them: "I know your works: you are neither cold nor hot. Would that you were cold or hot! So, because you are lukewarm, and neither cold nor hot, I will spew you out of my mouth" (Rev. 3:15-16).

One who is "lukewarm," lacking in interest and a zest for living, is a person who is denying his God-given opportunity to take the high road through life, denying the expression of his innate powers, and interfering with his progressive unfoldment of greater potentialities of mind and body.

We do not have to be limited to being just one of the crowd, trudging through life at a slow rate of progress, dying by degrees. By awakening our positive, powerful faculty of zeal, we can become not a follower, but a leader—not a plodder, but a radiant, enthusiastic exponent of the Christ zest for living.

The same amount of zeal has been given to all. How we accept it and how we work with it determine the way it will work for us—or against us. Zeal directed solely to selfish, human aims may consume us with its heat and friction. But enthusiasm developed as a spiritual attribute and dedicated to God's will and God's work will carry us to mountaintops of spiritual experience and help us immeasurably in the awakening of the other eleven powers.

Zeal works best for us when directed by the Christ, just as Simon, the disciple who represents this faculty, worked best and accomplished most after he chose to follow Jesus. Simon is described in two ways in The Gospels—as "the Cananaean," referring to his heritage, and as "the Zealot," referring to his activity before joining Jesus' disciples. Both descriptions give us an insight into the work of the zeal faculty before uniting with the Christ idea.

In the derivation of the name, the Cananaean (or Canaanite) is "one who exists in and for material things" (*MBD,* p. 136). The Zealots were a group of fanatics who lived in the mountains and fought the Romans, trying to free their country from foreign domination and restore self-government.

Before our zeal is awakened to spiritual ideas and rightly directed by the Spirit of God within us, it may dedicate itself solely to the pursuit of materialistic aims and goals. One may be zealous to make money, gain worldly power, or be successful in some materialistic project. This activity of zeal can serve as the awakening of enthusiasm and an interest in living. But, allowed to take over and dominate the individual's thinking, it may result in the fire that consumes and depletes, rather than provide a continuing supply of spiritual energy. Devotion only to materialistic goals sooner or later takes its toll.

Working for the worldly goal of self-government for the Jewish people, Simon became a Zealot. The Zealots were rough men—living a hard life, fighting continually, resisting, and resenting, but experiencing a sense of being filled with the flame of devotion to an ideal, the ideal of a free nation. As a Zealot, this man undoubtedly was filled with ardor, a great warmth of emotion for the cause he had chosen. But his efforts were devoted to forcing results in the material world.

Everyone needs something to feel strongly about. Everyone needs certain goals and aims that fight the inner fire. But when we learn to relate our goals first to the development of our inner powers and abilities under the Christ direction, then we have zeal working for us in a way that will fill us with spiritual energy to carry out our highest purposes.

Simon changed his way of life and became zealous for the Truth teaching when he made the decision to follow Jesus. And he was given all the energy he needed to fulfill his part of the divine plan in working with the other disciples. So zeal pours itself out as spiritual energy to follow through on the work of developing the whole man.

Simon the Zealot learned to give up force and fighting in order to cooperate with the other disciples under Jesus' direction. So the faculty of enthusiasm must spark and work with the other powers.

The name *Simon* means "one who hears and obeys." Simon, or zeal, works best when one hears the instruction of the Christ (as relayed through the wisdom center) and obeys that direction. Otherwise, even one's enthusiasm for Truth ideas may carry one away into outer activity. In speaking of the development of this attribute, Charles Fillmore warns: "Turn a portion of your zeal to do God's will to the establishing of His kingdom within you. Do not put all your enthusiasm into teaching, preaching, healing, and helping others; help yourself. . . . Do not let your zeal run away with your judgment" (*TM,* p. 133).

Zeal, then, is to be directed by judgment. Working without guidance, it is a fire that is uncontrolled, feeding on itself. Under the leadership of wisdom, tempered by love, it becomes a tremendous spiritual energy that carries the individual forward to greater and greater achievement. But it must be exercised first in a prayer way, transforming the inner man according to the spiritual pattern of the Christ.

When first awakened to spiritual ideas, we may be carried away in our desire to transform the world—or even just to change our family and friends. But we must learn to direct this energy first toward transforming ourselves, bringing forth our own spiritual nature. Our greatest influence on others will be the result of the changes we have made in ourselves.

Under no circumstances should our wonderful faculty of zeal be repressed. But it must be channeled to ignite the spiritual flame within us. That light will be a beacon to others. You will have the greatest ability to inspire others when you are alight with the radiance of your own Christ experience, brought about through dedication to prayer and spiritual realization.

Never judge zeal by the noise it makes. It functions best when it glows as the burning bush that Moses saw—radiating from within, without being consumed. Zeal that continually talks about being "excited" and trying to convert others exhausts itself in time. Enthusiasm that develops as an inner flame of devotion to the Christ idea continually generates energy to do God's will and work, always under the direction of the wisdom faculty.

The faculty of zeal makes its home at the base of the brain, at the back of the neck, in the medulla oblongata. From this center, it radiates energy to accomplish good. If this ardor is wrongly directed toward converting others by force or resisting and resenting in a human contest, it may bring about a stiff neck, or worse, an arthritic condition in the neck, resulting from too many years of determined force in behalf of a human cause.

In developing the faculty of zeal, it is important to remember to practice relaxation, because the zeal center is particularly receptive to tension. As you put your attention on the medulla oblongata, awakening your faculty of enthusiasm to spiritual activity, remind all the nerves and muscles in the back of your neck to relax. Let go and let God work. Say this over and over, *Relax. Let go and let God work.* The nerves and muscles of your body were created to serve you. When you continually remind them to relax, they will obey. But if you become carried away with enthusiasm and push for results, they may develop tensions that take over and continually call attention to themselves. You are not here to be intimidated by the demands of your body. You are here to develop and express your Christhood, and the body is designed to help you do it.

The power center at the root of the tongue and the zeal focal point at the back of the neck are both points through which tremendous energies can be released, but neither faculty has the know-how to govern and direct the power thus released. So both power and zeal must be guided to the right use of the spiritual energy they project. Remember this particularly as you awaken the zeal center. Keep the Christ, pouring out His wisdom to guide you, in charge. You need the fire of enthusiasm to become what you are designed to be in your highest spiritual nature, but you are to keep the spiritual reins in your own hands.

When you are filled with spiritual enthusiasm, you are joyous and energetic, your senses are quickened and awakened to new life, and you have a new feeling of being vitally alive.

To develop your spiritual realization of zeal, start with the intellectual approach and then build up your inner light and energy, always under the direction of the Christ.

1. Dissatisfaction

We will never become zealous about our spiritual growth and improvement if we are satisfied with things as they are. In considering the development of our zeal faculty, we must be sure to think in terms of divine dissatisfaction, rather than disgruntled discontent.

Perhaps we may first become dissatisfied because we feel there should be something better than we are now experiencing; but if we justify our dissatisfaction by blaming our troubles on other people, conditions, and situations, we will never even begin our climb up the ladder of developing spiritual zeal. We will simply wallow in the mire of our discontent.

Divine dissatisfaction approaches life without resistance against things as they are and without blame of persons or things. Instead, it recognizes that there is a Spirit within that is urging us on to something better. It is up to us to respond to this urge by taking steps to improve our situation. Thus, dissatisfaction with anything less than spiritual completion serves as a goal to push us into development of the inspired enthusiasm that will lift us to new heights of joy and accomplishment.

2. Desire

"The universal desire for achievement, giving its mighty impulse to all things, is divinely good" (*TM,* p. 131). Charles

Fillmore pointed to the innate desire of every person to experience more of God's good. As we learn to pay attention to the desires of our hearts and to interpret them correctly, we awaken a "mighty impulse" to go forward into a greater expression of our spiritual powers and abilities. This is a positive follow-up to our feeling of divine dissatisfaction.

In this step, we crystallize our inner urge on certain objectives, using the desires of our hearts to determine the direction our zeal should take. Of course, our greatest desire is always to experience more of God, but at this point in our spiritual unfoldment we may interpret it in different ways. Our developing zeal may lead us to seek mountaintop experiences in prayer, or it may draw us into a search for the peaceful trust exemplified by the person who wrote the Twenty-third Psalm. At any rate, our desires, rightly interpreted, will provide the objective on which zeal can feed and grow.

3. Dedication

At this point, our awakening desires become so important to us that we are willing to make an investment of ourselves in helping them to be fulfilled. We decide that our objectives are worth the price of our dedication and devotion to them, and for the spiritual awakening of our Simon faculty, we will choose goals related to the unfolding of our divine potentiality.

Here we make the decision that we will be like Simon in his greatest work, that of "one who hears and obeys" the leadership of the Christ within, our own spiritual nature. Like the disciple, we must make the decision to leave the Zealot way of the world, the method of trying to force results, and devote ourselves to the quieter, more orderly way of prayer and spiritual realization. If we are going to achieve true and lasting results, we will make this decision with a warm, glowing feeling, the beginning of spiritual zeal awakening in us.

4. Zeal

Divine dissatisfaction, the release of our deep-down desires of the Spirit, and dedication to the ideal of spiritual growth prepare us for the "inward fire of the soul that urges man onward . . . . Zeal is the mighty force that incites the winds, the tides, the storms; it urges the planet on its course, and spurs the ant to greater exertion" (*RW,* p. 216). We begin to feel the burning within us that is our motivation to "go forward."

Correctly established in wisdom and love and oriented to spiritual activity, the awakening power of zeal in us is the flame that burns but does not destroy. It drives us forward into the greater expression of our innate divinity. It even begins to generate the energy we need to accomplish the things that we need to. At last our zeal center is wide awake and functioning. Something beyond our intellectual decision is in charge and carrying us forward by its own propelling power.

5. Quickening

As spiritual zeal begins to do its work in us, it awakens not only new energies of the mind and soul, but also of the physical body. This is quickening, "an inflow of divine vitality into the body . . . . Spiritual quickening is a waking up of the whole man to the full consciousness of what he is in the sight of God" (*RW,* p. 161).

Mind and body, we have a new sense of being wide awake, vitalized, energized, renewed, on fire with spiritual purpose and determination. We find that we can expend superhuman effort without becoming weary. We are filled with a vital flame that not only energizes our life, but also serves as a radiant beacon, inspiring others to spiritual activity and growth. We are wide awake to our spiritual faculty of zeal and are sustained by its life-giving energy.

6. Genius

At this point one is so devoted to the spiritual ideal and so filled with the flame of inspiration that there is no concern about what others may think or how they may react to one's ideas of Truth. One does not try to impress anyone, but rather radiates that which one is and acts always from inner spirituality. The word *genius* comes from the Latin word meaning "guardian deity" and designates the person who is so in tune with the Spirit within that he continually displays exceptional powers. Jesus Christ was such a man. Fillmore says of him, "There have been men who have told us about God, but none who have demonstrated the wisdom and power of God as Jesus did" (*TM,* p. 137). We, too, would become the "spiritual genius in human form."

7. Energy

Complete development of our God-given potential of zeal results in a continuous, unfailing supply of energy. This is the result of our perfect spiritual unification with the Source. In this oneness, inspiration is no longer a conscious activity, but simply serves as the cause of the continuing release of vital power as needed.

Fillmore explains this outpouring of Spirit as "the power of God within us to accomplish . . . . Zeal in motion, the forerunner of every effect" (*RW,* p. 62-63). Complete realization of the faculty of spiritual zeal supplies all the vital energy we need for everything from prayer itself to physical accomplishment.

Instructions

Remember that all spiritual powers respond best to an attitude of relaxed expectancy. In developing the faculty of zeal, it is especially important to give the ganglionic center at the back of your neck the instruction to relax. In developing zeal you are, in a sense, "playing with fire." Fire can serve a useful purpose or it can burn and destroy. Zeal rooted in human thoughts and feelings, tense and anxious to have its own way, can only produce destructive results on your mind and body in the long run. Spiritually charged, this faculty burns without destroying in an attitude of relaxed expectancy of good.

The following affirmative thoughts will help you build this faculty, with its resultant outpouring of spiritual energy:

> Dissatisfaction: *Divine dissatisfaction awakens in me an urge toward spiritual growth.*
>
> Desire: *Desire impels me to seek spiritual understanding.*

Dedication: *With joyous expectancy, I dedicate myself to the will and the work of the Father within.*

Zeal: *The inward fire of spiritual zeal urges me on to greater experiences of God's good.*

Quickening: *I am quickened in mind and body by the compelling awareness of my own divinity.*

Genius: *I listen to God's voice within and act fearlessly and courageously at all times and under all circumstances.*

Energy: *I am unified with the energy of the universe.*

If, in the course of concentrating on the zeal center, you find that the back of your neck is becoming stiff or has a congested feeling, then stop and put your mind on something else. Until Simon is trained and completely dedicated to expressing the Christ only, he may have a tendency to revert to his role as the Zealot, enthusiastically seeking to promote his aims and goals by using force and resistance. Here zeal, under human direction and motivation, may insist on forcing ideas of Truth on others, "for their own good," of course, or pushing through a pet project for self-glorification or just tensing up the back of the neck with a sense of urgency in thinking.

It takes time and consecration to the Christ ideal to bring zeal to the point where it is not an expenditure of human energy to reach a human goal, but rather a joyous experience of oneness with Spirit, resulting in a continuing flow of energy to do God's will and God's work, with zeal guided always by the spiritually enlightened faculty of wisdom.

13

Let
Go
and
Grow

"**W**hen morning dawned, the angels urged Lot, saying, 'Arise, take your wife and your two daughters who are here, lest you be consumed in the punishment of the city.' But he lingered; so the men seized him and his wife and his two daughters by the hand, the Lord being merciful to him, and they brought him forth and set him outside the city. And when they had brought them forth, they said, 'Flee for your life; do not look back or stop anywhere in the valley; flee to the hills, lest you be consumed.' . . . But Lot's wife behind him looked back, and she became a pillar of salt" (Gen. 19:15-17, 26).

The story of Lot's wife is an extreme example of one who has failed to develop the God-given faculty of renunciation. Because this woman simply would not let go of her old life, even under the pressing emergency of the destruction of the two cities of Sodom and Gomorrah, she suffered not only mentally but physically. She missed her opportunity to start a new life in a new place.

Mentally, she was trying to hold onto the past, with all its negation, and her whole being was preserved in limitation as a result of it. (Salt was used in Old Testament times as a preservative.)

It is easy to fall into the pattern followed by Lot's wife, but if we are going to develop our spiritual faculties, we must include along with the others the power of renunciation, or elimination—the ability that enables us to cleanse and purify the whole being.

Some people in making a study of developing the new-person idea are more interested in using affirmations than denials. They may consider the whole concept of renunciation a negative rather than a positive approach. But this is not true.

Charles Fillmore explains: "It is just as necessary that one should learn to let go of thoughts, conditions, and substances in consciousness, body, and affairs, when they have served their purpose and one no longer needs them, as it is that one should lay hold of new ideas and new substances to meet one's daily requirements. Therefore it is very necessary that the eliminative faculty be quickened in one, and a right balance between receiving and giving, laying hold and letting go, be established" (*MBD,* pp. 652–653).

As elimination is necessary to the completion of the digestive process in the body, so renunciation is important to the completion of the establishment of divine order (the faculty centered in the digestive organs) and the fulfillment of wisdom (working from its throne in the pit of the stomach). As the heart and the organs of digestion work in close conjunction, love must also cooperate with the fulfillment of the functions of wisdom, order, and renunciation.

As the channel of elimination must be kept open if the body is to continue to receive nourishment, so the channels of mind power must be kept open for the digestion of greater ideas through the release of old, outworn, negative thoughts and feelings.

Circulation is the law of life in the physical body. It is the law of prosperity in the affairs. And it is a working principle in the development of the whole being, the spiritual person of the new age, with twelve basic attributes.

When we look at the whole picture, we see that one of our faculties must be the developed ability to release and let go in order to purify our minds and bodies and prepare the way for greater good to come in. In a sense, renunciation must work in conjunction with all of the faculties, as we replace old, wrong habits of thought and feeling with the new concepts and understanding that will be the basis for spiritual growth and development. As we would remove weeds from our flower or vegetable gardens in order to give the desired plants room to grow, so we must remove weed-thoughts from our minds to prepare room for our budding spiritual assets.

The disciple who represents the faculty of renunciation in Jesus' calling and training of the twelve is Judas Thaddaeus, also referred to as "Judas, the son of James" to distinguish him from Judas Iscariot. He is credited with being the author of the

Bible book of Jude, and some authorities believe he was the brother (not the son) of James, the disciple who represents order.

Thaddaeus makes his home in a ganglionic center near the base of the spinal column, from which he supervises the elimination of waste from the body, as well as the greater work of sorting and releasing thoughts and feelings that are not in keeping with the perfect-human idea being developed under the Christ direction. He works quietly, for the most part, supervising the activity of the organs of the lower digestive tract.

Not only are we to let go of all thoughts which are not in keeping with divine concepts—such as fear, doubt, and worry—but also we are to relinquish thoughts, concepts, and feelings which have been outgrown, even though they once served a useful purpose in our lives. From the story it would seem that Lot's wife loved her home and regretted leaving behind her material possessions, her friends, and her memories. But the fact she looked back instead of forward meant she was not ready for her greater good to come.

Perhaps we had a day of glory in the past that we recall from time to time to help compensate for feelings of shortcomings in the present. Looking back is no substitute for taking hold of life where we are. Maybe there have been relationships that in the past played an important part in our lives. It is good to give thanks for the happy times and occasions of sharing we have enjoyed, but if by looking back we miss the present, we are not fulfilling the purpose for which we were put here on earth: that of becoming the image and likeness of God in expression as well as in potential. So we must train this faculty to renounce, release, let go of all that does not belong to us as the awakening children of God we are designed to be.

The development of our Thaddaeus faculty in a spiritual way will benefit us mentally and spiritually, and it will bring about a transformation in our physical bodies. Purification of thought and feeling expresses itself as upliftment of the whole body consciousness, resulting in freedom from congestion and constipation, a lighter step, a divinely ordered adjustment of weight, a sparkle in the eyes, and a youthful complexion.

Heavy thoughts weighing on the mind cause heaviness in the body and coarseness in the skin. Remembrance of past hurts and injustice draws lines on the face and can produce a tense, strained look. We must eradicate all that would limit us in mind or body if we are to become the radiant Christ idea in expression.

Jesus was referring to this idea when he said, "If any man would come after me, let him deny himself and take up his cross daily and follow me" (Lk. 9:23).

Daily, hourly, momently, we must cross out and cleanse all thoughts, feelings, and memories that do not belong to us in our highest spiritual nature. This is the only way that we can follow Jesus in lifting up our twelve powers of mind and showing forth our Christ-nature through the whole person.

This crossing out or crucifixion of pet peeves, longtime grudges, deep angers, and resentments may be an excruciating process. The human soul is reluctant to give up those ingrained habits of thoughts and feelings that are established in consciousness. But it can be done, if we will awaken Thaddaeus and put him to work for us.

When Jesus spoke of denying the self in order to follow him in bringing forth our divine potential, he was not referring to a denial of our identity. Rather, he was telling us to withdraw our sustenance of thought and feeling from all that does not measure up to the divine pattern. This is Thaddaeus' job—sorting out our thoughts and feelings and releasing all that does not belong to us as children of God.

Thaddaeus works best when given charge of incoming messages to deny them before they gain a foothold. But our eliminative faculty is perfectly capable of cleansing even the deepest emotional and mental errors if we will give it a chance.

We have to deny and release the false or outworn concepts we may have chosen consciously. We also must wipe out the thoughts we have absorbed from the race consciousness (the collective subconscious) without knowing it. These beliefs in old age, death, poverty, and other human ills must be cleansed consciously, because they are so insidious that they may creep in the back door and find a foothold if we are not actively aware of them and if we do not consciously reject them. Charles Fillmore explains, "The beliefs that you and your ancestors have held in mind have become thought currents so strong that their course in you can be changed only by your resolute decision to entertain them no longer" (*TM,* p. 154).

Remember, with renunciation as with the development of the other powers, to maintain a relaxed, expectant attitude. If you try to use force to get rid of unwanted thoughts and feelings, they will fight right back. So simply put the Christ in charge, and in the authority of your spiritual nature, take command of your thinking and reject all that does not belong to you as a child of God, firmly and decisively, but with the relaxed expectation that those unwanted visitors will obey and leave.

We build our elimination faculty through stages: first, by training our thinking process; then, by awakening our spiritual ability to discriminate and cleanse our thinking-feeling nature; and finally, by purifying the whole being. The steps in developing our power of renunciation are these:

1. Awakening

Until we become aware of the errors we are making in our thinking-feeling processes and desire to cleanse and purify our whole being—mind, emotion, and body—we will do little to awaken Thaddaeus. But once we become awake to the importance of this God-given potential and see how the power of renunciation can serve us in the renewing of the whole person, then we are ready and eager to put it to work.

The word *awakening* is derived from Anglo-Saxon words meaning "to watch" and "to arise." Through watching, we become aware of our thoughts and feelings and begin to see the importance of sorting them out and cleansing those that do not belong to us in our spiritual nature. Then, arising, we make the decision to do something about it.

All great projects in our lives start with a decision, and the development of this spiritual faculty starts when we determine that we will take action to cleanse and purify our thinking-feeling nature. This leads naturally to the next step.

2. Repentance

Repentance is not, as many have thought, a concentration on the errors or sins of the past, with deep feelings of sorrow or regret. It is simply a turning away from the wrongs and refusing to give them continued support in thought and emotion. Once the thoughts and emotions that caused the error conditions are cleansed, our life begins to take a different direction.

Fillmore defines repentance simply as "a turning from a belief in sin and error to a belief in God and righteousness; a reversal of mind and heart in the direction of the All-Good" (*RW*, p. 167).

In order to accept God's forgiveness of past mistakes, we must turn away from them, stop dwelling on them, make what restitution we can, and then go on to build something better in mind. This is a conscious mental step.

3. Renunciation

Renunciation is a continuing process of denial. In order to become completely free of the past, we must go through a conscious procedure of mentally cleansing the error thoughts, the outgrown concepts, and the negative feelings that do not belong to us as children of God. Here we activate the law of giving and receiving—giving up the lesser in order to prepare room to receive the greater good.

Denial does not mean denying ourselves anything that is a part of our good experience in living. It does mean that we now take charge in our own minds, sort out the thoughts we find there, reject the ones that don't measure up to our chosen spiritual standards, and replace them with new, positive ideas of Truth.

In working our way through this mental step of renunciation, we must remind ourselves to be nonresistant. If we vehemently try to rid ourselves of unwanted thoughts and feelings, we will find that they become even more determined to stay. But if we quietly and gently take command of our minds and consciously refuse to give support to the things that do not belong to us as children of God, they will slip away for lack of nourishment.

4. Refinement

After we have taken the first three steps up in our mental awakening of the Thaddaeus faculty, we begin to see changes in ourselves. We look different. We think differently. We notice things that may have passed unnoticed before. We are passing through a level in which our whole being is refined, as metals and other substances are refined in the fire, freed from impurities and prepared for finishing in a new form.

Here we pass over the bridge to the spiritual awakening of the faculty of renunciation. Through our mental preparation, we started an activity that is now beginning to work in mind and body. We will find that as our thoughts are refined, our body also changes in appearance as the result of the refining process taking place in us; it works through our whole being.

5. Remission

Always when we have developed a faculty to a certain point, a spiritual activity takes hold and carries us forward, for the power of renunciation or elimination is the work of the grace of God, or remission.

Fillmore describes grace as "aid from God in the process of regeneration" (*RW,* p. 88). In Unity we understand grace as the forgiving love of God, which sets us free from past mistakes and the karmic results of those mistakes.

God's grace is free to all, but it can be consciously accepted only by those who have prepared to receive it by erasing errors in consciousness and building an inner ability to start fresh. God can only pour out His forgiving love in and through our lives when we have first forgiven ourselves, in the sense of giving new and greater concepts of good for the old error thinking.

As we come to this level of development, we are ready for the remission or pardon of past mistakes, and we can receive the cleansing outpouring of God's forgiving love, which sets us free to take another giant step forward.

6. Re-creation

"You have put off the old nature with its practices and have put on the new nature, which is being renewed in knowledge after the image of its creator" (Col. 3:9–10).

The spiritual activity of renunciation now becomes a continuing process of lifting up the whole person. Now that the Christ is in charge, wise choices are continually made in consciousness, so that only the good is allowed to enter, and the individual is renewed and transformed by a continuing purification of soul and body. Fillmore describes a re-creation or redemption as "a gradual transformation that takes place as man pays the price, gives up self, and allows Spirit to work in mind and body" (*RW,* p. 165).

Renunciation has become a working spiritual power.

7. Purity

Purity is the ultimate goal of the whole process of cleansing through which we have grown. It is the expression of oneness with Spirit in the realization of this attribute, so that there is no longer any need for conscious consideration of thoughts and feelings. There simply is nothing to which error can attach itself. There is oneness with the Source that results in identification with good only.

The person who has reached this stage was described by Jesus in the Beatitudes. He said, "Blessed are the pure in heart, for they shall see God" (Mt. 5:8).

In this state of consciousness, we do see God everywhere, because the spiritual working of renunciation has completely eliminated all error consciousness. There is nothing else to see; there is just God and good.

Instructions

As you develop this power, be sure to keep in mind that renunciation is not a negative, fighting activity, but a positive, nonresistant method by which we cleanse and purify the consciousness. By concentrating on the ganglionic center at the base of the spinal column, you not only will awaken Thaddaeus to help you in mental and emotional release, but you also will enlist him in the cleansing of your body through spiritual methods. Development of the power of renunciation brings tremendous benefit to the whole being.

Start with the intellectual awakening of the faculty and then let it unfold through the spiritual steps to oneness with the activity of Christ, resulting in the purity of the whole being.

The following are thoughts to use for the climb up the levels of renunciation:

> Awakening: *I am aroused to positive action to free myself from wrong thinking habits of the past.*
>
> Repentance: *I turn away from old habits of limited thinking. I know that God is unlimited.*
>
> Renunciation: *I constantly replace old error thoughts with new spiritual truths.*
>
> Refinement: *My mind and body are cleansed and purified as I refine my thinking.*
>
> Remission: *God's grace sets me free from mistakes of the past and the results of these mistakes.*
>
> Re-creation: *My whole being is continually renewed and transformed after the image of its Creator.*
>
> Purity: *With purity of heart I see God everywhere.*

Claim
God's
Gift of
Life

Many people, in considering the twelve disciples and the powers they represent in life, would like to forget about Judas Iscariot, the man who betrayed Jesus Christ. But Judas had a necessary role in the Messiah story, and the quality he represents—life—plays an important part in our development of the perfect-person idea.

Even though Judas committed suicide after he had betrayed Jesus, he wasn't out of the picture completely. After the Resurrection, the other eleven disciples met and chose a successor to Judas to bring their number back to twelve. So the faculty of life, operating on a higher plane, continues to work with the other powers for the lifting up of the whole being.

Charles Fillmore explains that Judas, or life, "carries the bag, he is the treasurer of our system, a thief also. He is selfish, proud, ambitious, tyrannical—but he cannot be spared. His faults must be overcome" (*MBD,* p. 376). In developing our God-given potential, we cannot ignore Judas. We must learn to recognize his weaknesses and limitations and cope with them by lifting the life idea to a higher plane of consciousness.

According to Fillmore, the surname *Iscariot* means "man of hostile encounters; man of conveniences," (*MBD,* p. 300) and this indicates Judas' tendency to be devious in his dealings, to put worldly considerations above spiritual insight, to try to take things into his own hands, even in dealing with Jesus.

Judas was the one who questioned Mary's anointing of Jesus' feet with precious ointment. He would have preferred that the ointment be sold and the money turned over to him, as treasurer of the group, to be "given to the poor" (Jn. 12:5).

Considering that when Judas betrayed Jesus to the authorities, there is a strong possibility that he was doing it in an effort to force Jesus to proclaim himself the Messiah and to establish his kingdom on earth. When the disciple discovered that his plan apparently had not worked, he tried to return the silver and reverse his actions. But it couldn't be done, and he showed his remorse and despair by killing himself.

Iscariot was a "man of conveniences" who was simply trying to get along in the world. But he was also something better. He was Judas, and his given name means "praise Jehovah" (*MBD,* pp. 372, 375). This man had to have some special spiritual qualities, or he would never have chosen to follow Jesus in the first place.

Fillmore explains: "Praise is the positive pole of life. Praise is the key to the increase of life activity" (*MBD,* p. 373). So we can learn to lift our Judas faculty of life by praising and giving thanks for life as a spiritual idea. We must deny sustenance to the side of our nature that is devious and unworthy and clothe ourselves in pure ideas which flood the whole body with the vitalizing "river of the water of life" (Rev. 22:1).

Judas makes his home at a center governing the generative or sexual organs. To awaken the life center, concentrate on a point just behind the top of the pubic bone. With your attention on this point, you can praise the pure life of Spirit into a healing flow to renew and revitalize your whole being. Remember, as with all of the powers, the life center serves merely as a point from which the awakened activity of the power pours through the whole being.

Fillmore says, "Once the word of the Lord is sown in any of these centers—the cells of which are like blank phonograph records—they take the thought that is given them, and send it through the whole organism" (*TM,* p. 19).

This is especially true of life. There is a center for the expression of life in each of the five octillion atoms of our physical body. Awakening the ganglionic center for life should not only activate the idea in mind, but it should also pour out a vitalizing, renewing flow of energy to awaken every atom to a new and greater expression of its potential. Visualize the river of life flowing forth from the life center to bring a new animation to the whole being.

All people are expressing the life idea to a greater or lesser degree, but only those who are keeping this power under the direction of the Christ can enjoy the fullness of life that is their God-given potential. We are to experience life as an idea that not only enriches the soul, but also lifts the physical body into a perfect expression of the pattern God implanted in it from the beginning.

Jesus so perfected his body that he could either use it on the physical plane or project it into another dimension. And Judas played his part in such a way that Jesus was given the opportunity to demonstrate his overcoming for all to see.

Judas represents the life idea that is wrapped up in itself and its demands and needs. It seeks sensation and personal gratification, instead of the good of the whole. Its false standards and the surrender to the demands of the senses result in a drain, rather than an increase in the life flow through the organism.

Judas may dissipate his life energy in a temper tantrum, as he allows the anger to take over and carry him away with it. Gluttony is another way in which Judas may rob the body, as he seeks satisfaction by overeating and generally letting his hungers govern him. Lustful indulgence of the sex urge is another way in which he allows himself to be carried away, substituting lust for love.

In the long run, with the Christ in charge of the unfoldment of the divine potential, Judas has to go, and he is replaced by Matthias, the disciple who joined the other eleven after the Resurrection. Matthias is "the lifting up of this faculty . . . that it may aid the individual in laying hold of his higher, spiritual attainments, even eternal life, through the power of his indwelling Christ" (*MBD,* p. 434).

The derivation of the name *Matthias* is the same as that of Matthew, another disciple who represents the will. In its highest sense, this name means "given wholly unto Jehovah," and both the will and the life idea must be devoted completely to the Christ idea for the final overcoming of limitation.

Neither life nor will is intelligent of itself, and both must be directed by wisdom, understanding, and love—all working under the direction of the spiritual-person idea. To lift Judas to the Matthias consciousness, we should also see that life works closely with another power which is located nearby, the Thaddaeus faculty of renunciation, with its center at the base of the spinal column.

It takes much cleansing to refine the life idea in soul and body. The selfishness and acquisitiveness of Iscariot must be purified. Life must learn to draw its own sustenance from the universe freely and easily, without the covetousness and hostility that close it in and limit it. Life works best when it is able to flow throughout the whole being as radiant energy, devoted to the Christ activity and governed by the Christ wisdom and order.

Never deny the life idea or think of any part of your body as unclean. Rather, awaken the life faculty at its center and then feel its animating action radiating through all the cells and atoms of your being as a greater expression of God. This is the way in which death of the physical body will finally be overcome.

Fillmore adds: "This resurrecting process is now going on in many people. It is a gradual change that brings about a complete transformation of the body through renewal of the mind. Spirit, soul, and body become unified with Christ Mind" (*TM,* p. 170).

To awaken your faculty of life to its spiritual potential, you may follow these steps of unfoldment:

1. Recognition

We must have a good understanding of and a good feeling about the life idea if we are to develop it as a useful servant. Life is our friend, not our enemy, and we are to cultivate it as a friend.

The word *recognition* is derived from the Latin words meaning "to know again." Here we begin to return in mind to the original idea of spiritual vitality and livingness. We remind ourselves of the reality that God-life is our life and that God's life energy is the power which animates our whole being.

Life may be Judas, making its selfish demands on us, seeming to deplete and exhaust us, but it can be elevated to become what it was designed to be, one of our spiritual assets. At this point we are training our thinking nature to know life in this way.

2. Sensation

Misunderstood and allowed to take control, sensation can become the serpent that misleads us. Raised and aroused to spiritual activity, sense impressions can help us to know and experience the life idea.

Fillmore remarks, "Sense consciousness betrays man every day, yet it would be unwise wholly to destroy it before its time, because at its foundation it is good" (*MBD,* p. 376).

In its right place, sensation helps us to be aware of a vital activity of the divine life idea in every cell and atom of our being.

At this point, we know it because we feel it. Sensation is not to be sought for its own sake, but is to be used by us as a means of experiencing the life activity in and through our whole Self—soul and body. This step is an awakening to the life idea in our feeling nature.

3. Appropriation

After we have readjusted our thinking about the life idea and have begun to feel a surge of the power in every cell and atom of our being, we can begin to consciously incorporate life into our minds and bodies. At the lower level, Judas represents self-appropriation, expressing itself as selfishness. But elevated he becomes spiritual appropriation, an ability to draw from the universe the life and substance of Spirit.

After Judas had left, Jesus shared with the other disciples what has become known as the Last Supper. He passed to them bread and wine, symbolizing his blood and body, which in turn stand for the spiritual gifts of life and substance. He was inviting them to share in the elevation of the whole person that he had experienced.

Fillmore explains, "To appropriate the word of Truth is to take the substance of the word into one's mind and heart" (*RW*, p. 15). So we appropriate thoughts of spiritual life and make them a part of our minds and bodies.

4. Transmutation

After we have done our work of mental and emotional preparation, we use our powers of praise and thanksgiving to begin the spiritual activity of conversion of our lower energies into higher energies. Here Judas is lifted to the role of Matthias, through thoughts and feelings of praise and prayer dedicated entirely to God.

Something begins to take place in our minds and bodies as we praise the Spirit that gives us life and give thanks for its divine activity within us. Even our hopes and aspirations, our desires and direction are transmuted and lifted up through the activity of praise. Fillmore says praise "opens the inner portals of the soul to the full and free inflow of spiritual light and aspiration" (*MBD,* p. 374). Something indefinable begins to happen in us.

5. Regeneration

Here the work in mind and body, accelerated by the process of transmutation, pays real dividends.

Not only is the soul transformed, but the body also takes on new life and energy. This is "a change in which abundant spiritual life, even eternal life, is incorporated into the body" (*RW,* p. 165). This is a spiritual rebirth or renewal that spreads through the whole person. Here the Judas-Matthias faculty works actively with the Thaddaeus power to cleanse all that is not in keeping with the spiritual life idea. Even the work of overcoming is easier, because a divine current flowing through the whole being is carrying us forward, cleansing, purifying, and lifting us, and bringing about the transformation that is necessary for us to take our role as the new creation expressing itself in a perfected physical body.

6. Resurrection

This is where, as Fillmore writes, "Spirit, soul, and body become unified with Christ Mind, and body and soul become immortal and incorruptible" (*TM,* p. 170).

We may have thought of the Resurrection as exclusively the property of Jesus Christ, but this is not what he told us. He pointed out that we are to follow him in the spiritual raising of the whole person. He meant it when he said, "You, therefore, must be perfect, as your heavenly Father is perfect" (Mt. 5:48). Speaking as the Christ, He also told us, "I am the resurrection and the life . . . whoever lives and believes in me shall never die" (Jn. 11:25–26). If we give direction of the life idea over to the Christ, we overcome death.

7. Immortality

As with all of the powers, there is a place where we realize the activity in a conscious oneness with the Source; for life, this is the state of immortality. In the realization of immortality, there is no thought of life or death. Life is. Life is all. Fillmore points out: "The human race on this planet will continue to die and be reborn until it learns the law of right living" (*TM,* p. 174).

Instructions

In developing your Judas-Matthias faculty, focus your attention first on the life center, awakening the life idea in consciousness, then feel the radiant energy pouring out through your whole body, bringing new vitality to every cell and atom of your being. Life is an idea in mind and an activity in body.

The statements for your progressive development of spiritual life are these:

Recognition: *My life is God-life—whole and free.*

Sensation: *I am alive, alert, awake, joyous, and enthusiastic about life and living.*

Appropriation: *I accept God's life as a pure stream, healing and harmonizing every part of my being.*

Transmutation: *I praise the Spirit that gives me life, and I give thanks for divine activity within me.*

Regeneration: *I am renewed, restored, and reborn through the activity of Christ in me.*

Resurrection: *I am lifted into eternal life by the Christ within my own being.*

Immortality: *I am alive eternally in God.*

Appreciate your gift of life. Praise it. Bless it. Give thanks for it, and you will find that the supply of life is unlimited and everlasting!

Meditation
for the
Twelve
Powers

Now it is time to compile your study of the individual powers into a meditation that can be used daily to increase your understanding of the activity of each one, to awaken the centers in your physical body, and to prepare to receive the spiritual outpouring of power in each of the twelve areas.

You will want to make your meditation flexible, so that you can continue to advance in the various levels of unfoldment for each of the faculties. So start by writing out the statement you are using for each of the powers. This will be the prayer for your next step up, in each case. Do this on file cards, one for each faculty. At the top of the card, put the name of the attribute and the location of the center. Then, in the middle of the card, write out the statement. It is good to use file cards, because they can be easily replaced as you move from one step to the next.

Do not be disturbed if you find that you are just starting the intellectual unfoldment of one power while you are working on the spiritual level for another activity. In the long run, with persistence and prayer, your God-given potential will be unfolded in all its facets.

Now, with your notes in order so that you can refer to them easily without breaking your train of concentration, seat yourself comfortably and relax as you turn to the Spirit within. The following is a suggested form to use for your meditation. Say to yourself, *"Be still, and know that I am God"* (Ps. 46:10).

Say it slowly, seeking to feel a response of stillness in every part of your being, stilling all thoughts and feelings, literally calling on all the intelligent atoms of your being to listen, to be receptive, and to know the Truth you are seeking to unfold. Be relaxed; don't try to force. Open yourself quietly to the thought, *I am one with God.* The I Am or Christ of you is God! Let this idea take hold in your mind.

Then put your attention on the I Am or Christ center at the crown of your head and awaken the flow of light from this point with the thought: *The Christ light is flowing through me now.*

From the point at the top of the head, visualize a clear stream of light coming in and spreading through your whole body. See it becoming brighter and brighter as you concentrate on the awakening of the Christ as the guiding light of your spiritual unfoldment. Then drop your thought to the great solar nerve center at the back of the heart and stomach and realize this prayer thought from the book *Christ Enthroned in Man* by Cora Fillmore:

I am now in the presence of pure Being, immersed in the Holy Spirit of life, love, and wisdom. I acknowledge Thy presence and power, O blessed Spirit. In Thy divine wisdom I now erase my mortal limitations, and from Thy pure substance of love I bring my world into manifestation according to Thy perfect law.

Let the realization spread through your whole being as you savor the idea of the divine Presence and Power now in charge of the unfoldment of all your faculties.

Feeling yourself bathed in spiritual light, turn your attention to the faith center at the middle of the head and use your statement for the faith faculty. Think of the center as actually responding—awakening to the activity of faith.

Follow through with the statements for each of the twelve powers, switching your thought to the appropriate center in each case and thinking of it as opening up a new and greater outpouring of spiritual activity. Do not hurry. Linger over each point until you feel a response, an activity taking place within you. After you have awakened the understanding center in the front brain, let your attention drop to the soles of your feet and hold this thought: *My feet are placed on the firm rock of understanding.*

Awaken the other centers in the following order, using your prayer thoughts for each one: strength (small of the back); wisdom (solar plexus, at the back of the heart and stomach); love (solar plexus); power (throat, at the root of the tongue); imagination (between the eyes); understanding (front brain, followed by the feet); will (front forehead); order (a point just behind the navel); zeal (the base of the brain, at the back of the neck); renunciation (base of the spinal column); and life (the ganglionic center behind the pubic bone, followed by a realization of life radiating to every atom of your being).

After you have completed the realization of each of the twelve faculties, rest for a moment in the light of your awakened spiritual consciousness. Then quietly say, "*Thank You, Father.*"

Use this complete meditation at least once a day, changing the prayer thoughts as you feel you are advancing step by step. For convenience, you may want to compile all of the statements and record them on a cassette recorder, so that you can be free simply to listen and concentrate on the sound of your own voice. Make sure that you update the cassette as you advance.

When you have completed your study of the twelve powers, go back and review them one by one. Unfolding your God-given potential is one of the greatest projects you will ever undertake and well worth the time and effort it requires. But it is a *continuing* process. It is only through studying and awakening the powers one by one that you will unfold the divine, perfect, beautiful being you are designed to be, shining forth in all the perfection with which God endowed you in the beginning.

About
the Author

Winifred Wilkinson Hausmann is an ordained Unity minister and the author of six books, including *Focus on Living,* published by Unity Books, *Miracle Power for Today,* published by Doubleday, and *Dealing With Stress Through Spiritual Methods,* published by Spiritual Resources Foundation. *Your God-Given Potential,* originally published in 1978, was written after fifteen years of study and practice of the twelve powers.

A graduate of Agnes Scott College, Hausmann served as minister of Unity of Little Rock (Arkansas) in 1957 and 1958 before becoming minister of what was then known as Unity Center of Cleveland (Ohio), where she served from 1958–1987 and is now minister *emeritus.* Winifred and her husband George co-founded an outreach ministry that is now the Unity Church of Christianity in Chesterland, Ohio.

Winifred served on the board of the Unity Ministers' Association and the Association of Unity Churches from 1965 to

1967. She has taught classes at Unity School of Christianity in Unity Village, Missouri, and has made lecture tours for Unity in England and Bermuda as well as throughout the United States.

Winifred officially retired in 1990. She lives in Euclid, Ohio, where she paints and guest-speaks upon request.